THOUGHTUARY

365 Daily Reflections to Help You Reset, Renew, and Reclaim Your Life

By Ed Goyette

Gadugi Media

THOUGHTUARY: 365 Daily Reflections to Help You Reset, Renew, and Reclaim Your Life

Published by Gadugi Media in the United States of America

ISBN-979-8-218-73036-9

Acknowledgements

Thoughtuary didn't start out as a book. It began as a personal challenge to write every morning for 30 days straight. But after those 30 days, the act of waking up, getting centered, and expressing what flowed became such an essential part of my day, that I just kept going. The writing deepened. The thoughts started arriving at all hours. And eventually, the words became what you're now holding in your hands.

For all the time, effort, and energy I poured into these pages, you simply wouldn't be holding this book if not for the presence, support, and inspiration of the incredible people around me.

Thank you to Chris and Mel Robbins. Your kindness, love, attention, friendship, and inspiration profoundly shaped both me and this work. I'm grateful for everything you are, and the incredible good you bring to the world.

To my beautiful wife & family: For five years you listened, read, and offered encouragement as our lives shaped this project. Thank you for giving me the space I needed to create and the love and closeness whenever we're together.

To EVERY member of Launch 1.0, you were my daily "why". The amount of encouragement, faith, and love that you showered upon this book left me humbled. So from my heart to yours, Thank you.

~ For my dad, Ed Sr., whose faith in me never wavered, who was always there in good times and bad, and showed me the power of sitting down with pen-in-hand, and just letting things flow.

And to Pam, my wife, who walked gently beside me while this was written, sharing every trial, success, pain, and joy that eventually ended up on these pages. I couldn't wish for a better partner in life.

Foreword

There are some books that tell you what or how and other books that invite you to pause or inquire. Thoughtuary by Ed Goyette is a beautiful invitation to do precisely the latter—to slow down, listen up, and connect more deeply with our own values.

And yet this book is not a how-to or self-help prescription. Instead, Thoughtuary is a collection of reflections designed to encourage a look within. A subtle but honest jab—to spark curiosity in what we believe. Through a special blend of daily thoughts or poems, this body of work promotes authenticity over achievement and serves as a guide not to get more, but to accept what is.

I appreciate the honesty of Ed's writing. He doesn't sugarcoat the underbelly of life or gloss over the truth. His words create a safe space, giving us room to honor where we are, to find ease in the struggle, and to see our humanness through the trees of humanity.

The wide range of topics from mindfulness to resilience to self-compassion neatly composed into daily passages offer the reader a chance to consistently adventure, inward. In this day and age, we all need help remembering to stop and listen—to ourselves and the world around us.

- Christopher Robbins

Introduction

This book was written first thing in the morning and in the middle of the night on note apps, backs of envelopes, and recorded in voice memos. It was written in parking lots and waiting rooms, in bed, and out in nature.

It wasn't written out of desire but a strange sense of desperation—a desperation to get into the world the thoughts that came in so strong and unexpectedly that they just had to be written down and shared.

So now it's yours to do with what you please.

Maybe the thoughts in these pages will resonate with you.
Or maybe you'll read them through a critical lens and be less than impressed. In either case, my hope is that at least one of them ends up meaning something to you or creates just the slightest of shifts in your perspective for the good.

Because if even just that happens, it will have been worth the effort.

- Ed Goyette

⸸ January 1

...the time for passively seeking your truth has long since passed.

Rule Your Awakening
It is one thing to wake up,
release the grip of the past,
and be glad to be alive.
It is another thing entirely
to Rule Your Awakening.

You were a child once.
You were led, directed,
and raised in the image of another.
But you're no longer a blank slate,
and the time for passively seeking your truth has long since passed.

Today.

Today is the day not to be raised, but to rise—
rise with purpose, focus, and in service of everything you were meant to be.
Rise in honor of the hardships you've overcome and the trials you've endured.
Rise with the trust and confidence in yourself to lead your life, live on your own terms, and never be led again.
You can seek advice, perspective, and strategy.
You can find support in counsel and a tribe.
But only you alone can rule your awakening.
It's your time.
Get to work.

Ask Yourself This...
What parts of my life am I prepared to take charge of right now, and what small things can I do to start?

January 2

How many things that you've obsessively worried about have come true?

I Know, But…

I know I should be grateful,
but I'm paralyzed by fear.
I know I can change my perspective,
but that seems all but impossible.
I know things have been worse,
but that's ancient history.
I know, I know, I know...
But, but, but.

The two voices in your head—
one grateful, light, and full of faith,
the other claiming to be the "realist"
who will keep you safe,
won't let anything slip,
or let you be caught off guard.

You know, the one keeping you awake at night.

So the question is:
How many things that you've obsessively worried about have come true?
The answer, I'm sure you'll find, is close to none.

On the flip side, how many times have things "just worked out" for some reason? I'm guessing more than you can count.

So the next time you're worrying, remember that things do tend to work out in ways we can never imagine, and the terrible fates we feel are almost certain rarely, if ever, come true.

Ask Yourself This…

How will I remind myself that things usually work out for the best when I start to slip into fear?

⸸ January 3

I want a lot for you. Yes, I really do.

For You
I want you to be happy, fulfilled, joyous, and content...
I want you to be fear-less, unapologetic, authentic, and inspired...
I want you to be loved, cherished, appreciated, and adored...
I want you to be peaceful, serene, balanced, and relaxed...
I want a lot for you. Yes, I really do.

So I hope the world does its part today and is kinder to you than it has to be.
I hope those near you realize the gift that you are and do something to express it.
I hope you can be a little kinder, gentler, and loving with yourself—finally seeing not the flaws but the beauty, and not the age but the wisdom.

But if nothing else, I hope this little note does what I intended it to do—and that's to make you pause and realize that you deserve every bit of the above. Because you most certainly do.

Ask Yourself This...
What can I do to remind myself to practice self-love, acceptance and understanding, especially when the world gives me none?

⸸ January 4

Don't worry if you're not crushing your goals and feel like you're falling behind.

Be Small

At some point, we all bought into the fantasy of perpetual growth. We convinced ourselves that human beings could defy the laws of nature and simply rise, without ever dipping, stalling, or faltering.

We're fine. All the time—or at least we should be.
Really?

Are human beings the only things in the universe that don't expand and contract constantly? Should every dip, regress, or need to stop, be a cause for alarm?

I don't think so. In fact, it's literally impossible.

So if you're not crushing your goals and feel like you're falling behind, please don't worry. It just means that like everything else that has ever existed, you can't expand forever, and sometimes you will naturally contract.

Accept this.
Accept where you are.
Release your expectations and stay focused.

Because just as it naturally contracted, your life has no choice but to inevitably, expand again.

Ask Yourself This…

Am I accepting of life's ups and downs, and if not, how will I?

⸸ January 5

...an overdue battle has just begun.

Tightness
Do you feel it?
That tightness?
That inner push and pull?
Knowing you have to move, but unable to get up?

It would be easy in this moment to call it fear (and maybe it is).
It would be easy in this moment to find lack and place blame.
It would be easy in this moment to use this as evidence that nothing will ever change.

But the reality is, it's simply proof that an overdue battle has just begun—
the battle between the uncertainty of the future you want,
and the truth of what's happened in the past.

One is aspirational, unwritten, and takes work you might not feel you're up for.
It's contingent upon you finding a new gear, learning new skills,
and pushing through barriers you might not even have defined yet.
The latter is unchangeable and set in stone—
a stone, by the way, that is holding you down.

So yes, this feeling you have right now makes sense,
but let there be no doubt—it's a very good sign.
A sign that's telling you,
it's time to move.

Ask Yourself This...
What steps will I take to overcome the things that are stopping me and learn skillsI need to accomplish my future goals?

January 6

Worthwhile ideas never die, and can always be rekindled if you try hard enough.

Building a Fire (or how to bring your ideas to life)

1. Start with the small stuff.
   Big ideas need time to ignite and grow, so start small and build slowly

2. Fan the embers with focused breath.
   Inspiring others into action requires persistence and determination.

3. Once you have a flame, be grateful, then *slowly* add bigger pieces.
   Even with momentum, rushing into big commitments too quickly can smother what you've built.

4. When you're ready for the big stuff, choose carefully.
   Not everyone will be ready for your message —so find the right fit.

5. Every fire needs constant attention.
   NEVER take anything for granted.

6. Even if the fire seems completely out, warm embers always remain.
   Worthwhile ideas never die; they just go back to step 1.

Ask Yourself This…
What practices or mindset shifts will I adopt to stay focused and relentless in my pursuit?

⸸ January 7

So be there.

When Your Child becomes a Young Adult
Just as you begin to understand the reality of life, your child is starting to believe the lies it tells.

Just as your priorities finally start to align with a greater purpose, they want nothing more than to look away and shed their innocence.

It's at this crossroad where the pain of parenting can be overwhelming, because you are both experiencing life-changing awakenings, but in polar opposite directions. You, finally understanding life's deep truths, are forced to watch helplessly as they head into the world to learn them for themselves.

So be there.

Be there to help them when they need it,
but learn the restraint to wait for them to ask.

Be there to help them celebrate the victories
and pick up the pieces when they fail—
but only after they've first had the opportunity to do it on their own.

The faster you accept your new role in their life as trusted advisor, consultant, and coach, the longer you will stay deeply connected.

And that is one of the greatest blessings you could ever hope for.

Ask Yourself This…
How do I maintain and strengthen the connection with my child through this period of separation?

⸸ January 8

My uniqueness is a strength.

Pegs and Holes
I've always felt like a round peg in a square hole.
Some parts fitting in, but most not—which always left me struggling for acceptance from the better-fitting pegs, or looking for other holes.

When I thought I understood the hole and did what it took to fit in,
I ended up scraping the edges in what felt like the worst of ways.

I overthought things before I said them, then regretted the things I said, thinking I made a misstep or could've done better.

Deep down I knew this was untrue, that my uniqueness was a strength—not something to be embarrassed by or, worse, hidden altogether.

But I did both for as long as I can remember, which caused me to navigate so much alone. Things that, ironically, others found amazing, inspiring, and sometimes even impossible.

So I'm sitting here thinking that the walls need to come down even more, that the pegs and holes are not made of stone. And just maybe, that fully releasing the past, finally accepting my truth, and understanding that I'm not the only one who feels this way, just might make all the difference in the world.

Does any of this sound familiar? And if so, are you with me?

Ask Yourself This…
What steps will I take to let go of past experiences and embrace my true self?

⸸ January 9

Life isn't a competition.

Maintaining
Sometimes your highest aspiration isn't to achieve, crush, or expand, but simply maintain—and that's completely fine.

But seeing others constantly moving forward while you are standing still can take its toll.

Suddenly it feels like your goal to maintain what is good in your life in the face of whatever adversity you're going through is nothing but stagnation. That if you're not "moving forward" you're somehow falling behind.

This isn't true. Life isn't a competition.

The fact is that sometimes the best you can do is simply hold on to what you have. And not falling further, or letting your current circumstances get the best of you, is all you have enough for.

And that's ok.

So if you're just holding on and find that maintaining where you are is the best you can do, please understand that it's just fine.
Because when the day comes that you're ready to move,
you'll be so grateful that you maintained
and didn't fall.

Ask Yourself This…
How can I remind myself to appreciate what I have, and keep it top of mind?

⸸ January 10

There is more time for "the doing" tomorrow.

The Rest Between Notes
In a song, just as important as the notes being played are the rests between them—the pauses that let the listener process, appreciate, and grasp the meaning behind the music.

Life works the same way.

The rest, reflection, appreciation, and understanding can't truly happen while we're still in motion—because we flourish more in the pause than in the doing.
We make more progress after we've disengaged and allowed ourselves to simply "be."

So if today just feels like an ordinary day, accept it as that necessary pause—the space between moments of activity that keeps your life from becoming a chaotic string of disconnected notes.

Then honor it for the balance it brings.

Relax, enjoy, be bored if you need to—but never regret that you "didn't get anything done."

There will be plenty of keys to strike and beats to play tomorrow. But for today, the rest between notes might be exactly what you need.

Ask Yourself This…
How will I remind myself to shift my mindset to appreciate and embrace the "rest between notes"?

January 11

Discover the inner joy that is dependent on nobody but you.

Find a Way
There is no “right way” in life.
There’s not just one path to happiness or a formula for joy.
We are all wanderers,
blazers of our own trails,
and seekers of our own personal divinities.

So if you find yourself comparing, judging,
and seeing your life as something smaller than the miracle it is,
Please stop and appreciate the fact that you’re living a life like no other in history.
That this life, your life, is not only worth living but has a purpose far greater than you could ever imagine.

So find a way—a way to live on your terms, in service of your own dreams, and above all, true to your own heart.

Find a way to discover the inner joy that depends on nobody but you.
Yes, you will need more patience, self-love, and compassion than you might believe possible.
Yes, you’ll have to accept the hard times and honor the journey for what it is.

But never stop trying to find a way,
because I promise, if you keep searching,
it’s there to be found.

Ask Yourself This...
What expectations or comparisons keep me from finding a way?

⸸ January 12

Maybe it's because you've never truly listened to yourself with the rapt attention you give to others.

Permission to Speak

Many of us go through life thinking we have nothing of value to say. We look to others for perspective, accept their words as "wisdom," and wonder why we can never seem to rise to that same level of clarity.

The truth is, you have more to say than you can imagine,
and possess an inherent brilliance that has yet to surface.
Why? Simply because you've never given yourself permission to speak.

Maybe it's because you've never truly listened to yourself with the rapt attention you give to others.

Maybe you've never fully accepted the weight of your words or the depth of your experience.

But perhaps the most tragic thing of all is that you've probably never stopped to consider the incredible positive impact you could make if you simply opened your mouth, and shared your truth.

Perhaps "never" is too strong a word.
Perhaps you've tried.
But if you're still feeling small or insignificant in comparison to others, then you haven't fully given yourself the permission you so rightly deserve.

So please, take a moment and give yourself that permission.
Because what a tragedy it would be if we never got to look to you for perspective, and accept your words for the wisdom they are.

Ask Yourself This ...

What positive impact could come from giving myself permission to speak and sharing my truth?

⸸ January 13

Experience life minute by minute, without expectation and devoid of judgment.

The Other Shoe

For most of my life, I found it impossible to truly enjoy the good times because I was always waiting for "the other shoe to drop."

What an odd phrase. Because if you think about it, it's impossible to move forward without both shoes constantly rising and falling.
Good times depend on bad times that depend on good times...

That's life.
We live, struggle, learn, and progress.
Again and again and again.

The problem is that while we all understand this universal truth,
we have no idea how or when things will change, and worse, to what extent.
Since our minds exist to identify threats and keep us safe and crave rhythm and predictability, the end result is inevitably *fear.*

So how do we work around something so hard-wired into us?
When you're riding high, enjoy the abundance,
and acknowledge the upper end of the contrast between your normal existence and the good fortune you're having.

And when the "other shoe" does drop,
have faith that even in dark times,
there will be gifts to share and lessons to be had.

But above all, have faith that life always finds a way,
to raise the other shoe.

Ask Yourself This...

How often do I wait for "the other shoe to drop," and how does it impact my ability to enjoy the present?

⸸ January 14

I want you to think about what you're hiding.

You and Neil Peart (One of the greatest drummers of all time)
When Neil Peart was in high school, he was an awkward introvert with hardly any friends. He also had a passion for drumming and writing.

He saw drumming and writing as his ticket to acceptance, so instead of going to parties, he poured himself into them and eventually became one of the greatest rock drummers and lyricists of all time.

The irony is that his introversion never changed.
When all the parties, friends, and acceptance finally arrived, he wanted none of it. So he figured out how to bring his art to the world in a way that worked for him, set tight boundaries, then changed the world.

So, how does this relate to you?

I want you to think about what you're hiding or holding back.
Think about the things you're afraid to show the world because you're afraid they're not good enough, or what people will say.

Then think about Neil, pounding on his craft, constantly perfecting it, and taking the stage night after night on his own terms, spreading joy to the masses like he was born to do.

Now take a breath. If you're feeling the need to express yourself, there's a reason, and that just might be that someone, somewhere, desperately needs to hear what you have to say in a way that only *you* can say it.

So please, be like Neil, and honor that - on your own terms.

Ask Yourself This...
How can I use Neil Peart's journey as inspiration to push through my insecurities and share my gifts?

⸸ January 15

The truth is that you're vibrating on the same exact frequency as millions of other people.

A Million Answers to Your Prayers

Why is it that we can freely talk to God, pouring out our hopes and dreams, yet hesitate to ask each other for even the smallest things?
Isn't that why we're here—
to lift each other up, collaborate,
and help make each other's highest purpose a reality?

The truth is that you're vibrating on the same exact frequency as millions of other people.

Those are the people who align with you,
who will stand behind your purpose,
and help transform your dreams into reality.

So embrace vulnerability.
Take a leap of faith and reach out to someone you resonate with.

Invite them for coffee, or to simply share a moment.
Because you never know,
it just might be Divinely inspired.

Ask Yourself This...

What is one way I can expand my community to bring my dreams to life through finding a community of like-minded people?

⸸ January 16

So open your mind and learn.

Be the Honor Student
You can sit in a classroom,
but if you're staring out the window,
you'll learn nothing.

The same goes for life.

If you're not paying attention,
if you're letting the days go by without reflection,
if you're not examining the lessons being taught,
then when it comes time to be tested,
you'll most likely fail.

So open your mind and learn.
Open your eyes and see.
Open your ears and listen.
Open your heart and feel.

Class is in session—
So open your life,
and truly live.

Ask Yourself This...
What is one step I will take today to ensure I'm present enough to apply what life has taught me?

⸸ January 17

The words that we really need to hear.

Quote Your Own Heart
You can use the words of others to impress;
but the wisest words,
the truest words,
the words that we really need to hear—
can only be said by you.

So today, please listen carefully to what your heart is saying.
Then share it.
Do us all the honor of quoting your own heart,
because I can assure you,
We're listening

Ask Yourself This...
What messages from my heart have I hesitated to share with others?

January 18

How often do you prioritize the tiny and insignificant over what's truly important?

"Little bit Sasquatch is in wheelchairs but defend it for just being oh?"
This is a voice to text of a thought "I just had to get down right away". Something that hit me out of the blue that I felt was significant enough to quickly open the app and speak it at a stoplight.

What I should have done was take a couple of minutes
to pull over and ensure it was done right.

I didn't honor the gift
I trusted something unreliable with something irreplaceable.
I put the fear of being a minute late, ahead of the need to express something important.

How often do you prioritize the tiny and insignificant over what's truly important?
How many of your dreams, "I love you's", ideas, hugs, and kisses never happened because "You had to _____ first?"

I really hope "Little bit Sasquatch is in wheelchairs but defend it for just being oh?" resonates with you today,
because when I said it out loud at that stoplight,
I thought it was life changing.

Ask Yourself This...
What is one way I can remind myself daily to honor and express what is important without fear holding me back?

⸸ January 19

That's where life is truly lived.

Go Big or Go Home?
I'll go home.
That's where what's important is.
That's where connection happens.
That's where life is truly lived.
So I'll gladly leave the "going big" to others,
while I stay grounded, connect deeply
and build my thing, one small bit at a time.

Ask Yourself This...
What is one way I will stay grounded and prioritize what truly matters?

January 20

...each time, you, with all your imperfections, were God's perfect solution.

You are the Answer
Before you were born,
Somebody prayed with all they had for a child to arrive—
and God's answer was you.
Since then, many people have prayed
for someone to love,
someone to hold,
and someone to show up in their lives to make it better.
And each time, you, with all your imperfections,
were God's perfect solution.

So the next time you're feeling like your life isn't what it's supposed to be, just remember that you have been, and will always be,
God's answer to someone's prayers.

Ask Yourself This...
How does it feel to know that I am the answer to someone's prayers?

⸸ January 21

...you'll learn some beautiful things about yourself.

Know Thyself Deeply (in just 15 minutes)
Scroll back one year in your social media feeds.
And look consciously and critically at what you've posted.

Then, based on what you see, ask yourself:
What does it say about my worldview?
What does it say about what's important to me?
What does it say about who I am?

But most importantly,
Who is the person I'm showing to the world?
And what does that say about how true I'm being
to myself and others?

Ask Yourself This...
When will I scroll back in my feeds with a curious mind and open heart and think about what I discover?

⸸ January 22

Allow yourself to be the person you were meant to be.

Evolve

Personal evolution requires no willpower, motivation, inspiration, or force.
It comes from letting go, falling into, trusting, and experiencing pain… sometimes lots of pain.
It starts by going backward, not forward.
It comes from deep within.
It's when that soft but powerful voice whispers in your ear, "It's time."

So stop wasting time on "New Life" Mondays.
Stop trying to force yourself to change.
Instead, focus on slowing down,
quieting the noise, and loving yourself.
Love yourself so deeply that you'll no longer accept self-sabotage,
unhealthy habits, and negativity in your life.

I know—it's easier said than done.
But honestly, you have no choice.
Because it's only by doing this that the whisper has any chance of surfacing.
So please, know yourself, love yourself, and heal yourself.
Go back, go deep, unravel, open, and accept.
And allow yourself to be the person you were meant to be.

Ask Yourself This...

In what ways will I show myself more love, acceptance, and compassion as I heal and evolve?

⸸ January 23

We need all of you (yes, we truly do.)

Please Keep Going
This is important for you to know—
Someone is always listening.
More people care than you could ever imagine.
Life does get better.
You matter.
Your life has a purpose you may not know yet.
You could never be a burden.
We need you (Yes, we truly do).
So please, Just keep going.

Ask Yourself This…
Will I finally accept that I am not alone, I matter, and that there are people who need me more than I could imagine?

⸸ January 24

Water will always find a way.

Be Water
Tough as nails,
hard as steel,
solid as a rock…
All these are things we're told we should be if we want to survive in the world.
Me? I'll take water.

Water doesn't resist, it adapts.
Water doesn't break, it transforms.
And water will ALWAYS become still enough to reflect light back into the world, regardless of the size of the storm it's in or how long it lasts.

But water is anything but weak.
Water is a force to be reckoned with.
Water is relentless, perseveres, and never stops.

Yes, there are times when you need to stand your ground.
There are times that call for solidity and resolve in the face of adversity.
But I'll still take water.
Because at the end of the day,
nails will rust,
steel will break down,
and rocks will turn to silt.
But water will always find a way.

Ask Yourself This...
How can I remind myself to be more like water in my daily life?

⸸ January 25

Be the first to let someone know.

Start the Standing Ovation!

The next time you're moved, touched, or inspired,
don't hesitate!
Stand! Yell! Applaud!

Be the first to show someone they connected with you,
that all their hard work, passion, and sacrifice was worth it,
and that they succeeded in what they came there to do.

So start the standing ovation!
It will matter to them more than you'll ever know.

Ask Yourself This...
The last time I was moved by someone's work, did I take the opportunity to acknowledge and appreciate it?
If not, why?

⸸ January 26

We need to learn how to talk to each other again.

Disconnected
Isn't it ironic? Living in the most "connected" time in world history, yet feeling more alone than you ever have?

You notice even engaging online interactions feel hollow:
No eye contact.
No presence.
No real connection .
And though there are people you like and care about
on the other side of the screen,
they always seem so distant, as if they're not real.

Why then when you're with someone in person,
you find yourself drawn away from them and into your phone?
It doesn't make sense.

So maybe it's time you changed this
Start by doing these three simple things:
Commit to finding more ways to connect in-person
Be curious and start asking more questions
And when you're with someone, keep your phone out of site

Start there, and you'll find that soon,
you won't feel so alone anymore.

Ask Yourself This…
What will I do to become more curious about others today?

January 27

I'm not talking about financial equality.

What They Need
Life isn't about you getting what you want—
It's about helping others get what they need.

I'm not just talking about money,
but a shift from constant gathering to consistent giving of time,
perspectives, and expertise.

I truly believe that openness, selflessness, and connection can change the world, and the good news is that I see it happening more every day.

So, my question to you is:
Will you spend another day simply gathering,
or will you do your part to change the world
and give?

Ask Yourself This...
What is one way I can shift from constant gathering to consistently giving, and how would that make me feel?

⸸ January 28

This one isn't just a thought, it's a plea.

Push Your Limits
Today, you can choose to passively accept the negativity around you, or you can be the proof that positivity is alive and well.

The decision is yours:
Retreat in fear, or push the limits of your capacity for kindness, compassion, understanding, love, hope, and, above all, faith.

Can you imagine what would happen if you lived as if it's solely up to you to prove that good exists?
Damn.

NOTE
This isn't just a thought; it's a plea. Your smile, unexpected kindness, openness, and unique ability to uplift others are more powerful than you can ever imagine. So please, be the proof we need. Push your limits.

Ask Yourself This...
When have I retreated instead of embracing the opportunity to make a positive impact? How will I change that?

⸸ January 29

Never underestimate the power of fear.

Unconditional Fear
Fear is absolute, unwavering, and deadly.
It darkens the mind and tarnishes the soul.
It takes what should be yours and holds it just out of reach.
Fear moves faster than hope and goes even deeper than love.
Always present, it watches and waits—
trigger finger trembling, lip snarled—
ready to take you down before you even know there's a fight.

Know this about your enemy:
understand its power and purpose.
Study the scars it's left on your life;
Remember the dreams that were no match for its fury,
and the hopes that never had a chance to rise.
Never underestimate the power of fear.
Know the fear in you so completely that you can sense its presence even before it has a chance to attack.

Then, and only then, will fear not be the thing that drags you into darkness,
but a beacon alighting the path of opportunity before you.

Fear is insidious and holds you back from the life you're meant to live. But with immediate action, you CAN move past the paralysis it brings, and over time, turn your greatest enemy into the most powerful weapon you'll ever have.

Ask Yourself This...
How will I remind myself that I can use fear to my benefit when it starts to arise?

January 30

...life isn't a puzzle.

Masterpiece
Sometimes life seems like a huge puzzle with pieces scattered everywhere—pieces you're constantly trying to assemble into a picture called "The Life of Your Dreams."

But no matter how hard you try, the puzzle always seems to have pieces missing. The truth is, it will never be finished —
because life isn't a *puzzle*; it's a *painting.*

It's a never-ending work in progress—
strokes of brilliance, painful mistakes, soaring inspiration,
and depths of despair, but above all, truth.

So approach your life with the intention of creating a masterpiece,
stroke by stroke, and with time,
you surely will.

Ask Yourself This...
How will I remind myself to find joy in the ongoing creation of my life's masterpiece instead of waiting for it to be finished?

⸸ January 31

All you are and meant to be.

The Things That Surface
That honesty,
that tear,
that "I love you,"
that laughter,
that pain—
that stuff that keeps trying to surface,
that stuff you keep pushing back down,
holding onto,
never expressing.

It's time to let it break the surface, see the light, and be known.
It's time to breathe honest breaths,
speak words that are true,
and let the tears do what tears do best—
heal, release, and express what you're really feeling deep inside.

It's time to be you—
all you are and meant to be.
So laugh, love, and live without apology, denial, or shame.
We've always needed the real you.
What a gift it would be
to finally see it.

Ask Yourself This...
What feelings or thoughts have I been keeping inside? Why?

⳩ February 1

The contrast between your expectations and reality is the source of all your stress.
So please take a deep breath, release it, and enter the day open to what will be.

Ask Yourself This…
How can I start each day with openness and acceptance?
When will I start?

⸸ February 2

So I heard about this person, you know, called "The Real You."

Life Is Too Short To Stay Hidden
I know a guy called "The Real Me."
He's a bit different and has some thoughts you might consider strange.

He forgets many things he's said and plans he's made,
and feels he's at his best when he's connecting with people.

He has zero tolerance for negativity, gets choked up at the oddest things,
and sometimes says things around the house that are so bizarre
that his daughter kept a list called "Strange Things Uttered by My Father."

He also wants to inspire people to show their authentic selves to the world.

Why?

Because he knows life is too short to stay hidden,
and it pains him to see people living in fear of what others might think
if they knew "the real them."

So what does "The Real You" look like, and how can you begin to embrace that truth in a way that works for you?

Ask Yourself This…
What is beautiful about me, and why am I not showing it to the world?

⸸ February 3

...in a few years you'll trade anything to get this moment back.

Cardboard Castles

I know you're tired, and the last thing you think you want to do right now is play pretend with your kid.
But trust me, in a few years you'll trade anything to get this moment back.
Go build that cardboard castle....

Ask Yourself This...

Knowing time with my child is fleeting, how will I shift my perspective, prioritize quality time with my child , and appreciate the present?

⸸ February 4

Follow Your Heart.
It always knows
the best way to get you
to where you're going.

Ask Yourself This…

What is one thing I will do to start connecting more with my heart and less with my mind?

February 5

If your last name is Jones, I apologize.

About the Joneses
The Joneses are far from perfect.
In fact, their life is most likely in worse shape than yours.
They've just become experts at hiding it.
So never try to keep up with the Joneses—
Because you might just end up like them…

And if your last name is Jones, I apologize. I'm sure your life is just fine. It's just that somewhere down the line, some very wealthy family with your namesake set a bunch of unattainable standards for house size, lawn greenness, and vehicle choice—and people kinda noticed.

(If you are indeed that family of Joneses, you might want to ask yourself what's missing in your life that you're trying to make up for with all that stuff. Answer that question, and you might just find the thing you've really wanted all along—an abundance of happiness.)

Ask Yourself This...
What truly makes me happy, and how can I focus on those things instead of trying to meet society's expectations?

⸸ February 6

What you do with it is up to you.

All You Are
Every moment, you are moving farther away from and closer to Divine Love.
Away from its purest expression at birth and closer to a reunion with it at death.

Your life then is simply the connection of one to the other.

Time away from the divine to express what you've learned and who you've become.

Your birth gave you the power to expand the flow of love into the universe or even break it completely.

What you do with it is up to you.

The Beatles said, "Love is all you need."
I would expand it to say, "Love is all you are, love is all you've ever been, and love is all you'll ever be."

So please accept this about yourself (and everyone else for that matter), because your divinity is not just personal; it's universal.

Ask Yourself This...
How can I begin living in a way that honors my connection to Divine Love, recognizing it in myself and in others?

♰ February 7

It doesn't matter how you get to that place of peace, as long as you get there.

Meditation for a Restless Mind
My mind usually feels like it's racing in all directions—filled with distractions, random thoughts, and endless energy.

So, when I first started meditating, I found it hard to quiet my mind and focus on what truly mattered.
So I created a method of meditation that works for me.

First, I bought the birthstones of each member of my family.
Holding something tangible that represents the person I'm focusing on really helps me center my attention.

Then, to keep my mind from wandering, I created a simple phrase that captures the core of what I want to express for each person.
This combination of holding the stones and having a structured intention keeps me grounded.

I move from one stone to the next, and by the time I reach my own, I've settled into a deep sense of calm, allowing me to let go, be still, and breathe.

Remember, It doesn't matter how you get to your place of peace.
So find your own way, and go there..

Ask Yourself This...
How can I personalize my meditation practice to better suit my own mind and bring calm into my day?

⚕ February 8

Focus on the reality of the here and now.

Small Wins, Tiny Blessings
Today, be sure to take a break from obsessing over your problems, and take at least a few moments to stop and focus on the small wins, tiny blessings, and the things that are going well.

Yes, once again I'm talking about gratitude in the face of uncertainty, embracing the beauty of the here and now, and putting down the "what ifs" and "whens" for a while.

Do this, and I promise your day will be better.
So chin up, breathe, and release.
You've got today.

Ask Yourself This...
How can I remember to stop, take a deep breath, and let go of worries and experience the peace of the moment?

February 9

The Struggle is Real, But So Are the Blessings. Honor Them Both.

Ask Yourself This...

When will I finally shift my mindset to acknowledge and appreciate the blessings in my life instead of just focusing on my struggles?

⸸ February 10

...be honest about how you're doing.

Be Weird Today
When did it become "weird" to
sit, breathe, & mediate,
and "normal" to be stressed, busy, and overworked?

When did it become "weird" to share your feelings and
be honest about how you're doing
and "normal" to be closed off and always say you're fine?

I think it's time to reverse "weird" and "normal"
and be comfortable being honest with ourselves
and each other.

Wouldn't you agree? And more importantly, will you finally start being "weird"?"

Ask Yourself This...
How can I help others feel safe to share their feelings and experiences without worrying about being judged, while also being vulnerable enough to share my own feelings?

⸸ February 11

You are the very next link in the chain...

Share the Good
Your decisions whether or not to share
what you hear, think, and feel have the potential
to make a massive impact on the world

You are the very next link in the chain—
A connector of thought from one to another
So be mindful of the power of the words you use
Break the chains of negativity that come your way
and be the very strongest link in the chain of goodness

Ask Yourself This...
How can I actively seek opportunities to share acts of kindness, love, and support, amplifying the good and contributing to a chain of positivity in the world?

⸸ February 12

We need your crazy, your nuts, and especially your weird.

Hiding

Do you feel you're not living the life you were meant to live?
Are you hiding your greatness to be acceptable to those who are denying theirs, holding back because you're nervous about what other people would think if they saw the real you?

If this rings true, then you're actually showing up in the world as someone who doesn't truly exist? And this is keeping you from the friendships, love, and happiness your authentic self is truly meant to have?

Why are you doing this?

For the acceptance of people you're not aligned with anyway?
To stay on a path that leads you AWAY from fulfillment and to keep you doubting yourself 24/7/365? It simply doesn't make sense.

The truth is that we need you
The real you
The unfiltered you
We need it all -
Your thoughts, perspectives, passion, and energy.
We need your crazy, your nuts, and especially your weird
Because most likely, we're much more like you than you think.

So please take that leap of faith and share your authentic self with us!
If you do, I promise we won't let you down

Ask Yourself This...

In what ways am I currently holding back and not fully expressing my authentic self in various areas of my life?

⸸ February 13

The Formula for Personal Growth

Adjust.

Accept.

Learn.

Move On.

Repeat.

Ask Yourself This...
How can I remember to use this formula in my daily life to make the changes I want to see in my life happen?

⸸ February 14

...there's a lot about you to love.

What do you love about yourself?
No seriously.
I'd like for you to take the time right now to come up with a list
Dig deep.
Because there's a lot about you to love,
I'm sure of it.

Ask Yourself This...
What are some of the things I genuinely love about myself?

February 15

On water and thirst.

About that glass...
Whether we see the glass as half empty or half full usually depends on if the level rose or fell just before the water became still (and of course, how thirsty you *think* you are at the time).

Ask Yourself This...
How do I remind myself that perspective is indeed everything in my daily life?

⸸ February 16

Give right now.

Giving
What we have to give doesn't matter
whether it be money, time, a smile
or even just a positive thought or prayer.

The important thing is to give everyday.
In fact, you can give right now.
Just take a moment, and send a healing thought
to someone who needs it.
It's as simple as that.

Ask Yourself This...
How will I make giving a daily habit by focusing on sharing intangible gifts like love, support, and positive energy?

February 17

We're given thousands of miracles a day.

The Act of Standing
I stood up today.
It took about 2 Seconds for me to go from sitting
to be completely upright and ready to move.
In those two seconds,
I felt the muscles in my thighs tighten
my calves flex and push,
and the power transfer from my hips to my feet.

Finally, I felt all of the tiny adjustments that were being made to balance my weight perfectly over my feet.

It was just two seconds—
but the miracle of what had just occurred wasn't lost on me.
Because I knew in that very moment there were millions of people who would give anything to feel what I'd just felt—
knowing that with an almost imperceivable next thought,
they'd be walking across the floor just like I would be in a moment.

We're given thousands of miracles a day,
and all we have to do is be present to experience them.
How amazing is that?

So stop and appreciate the next time you stand up.
If not for the miracle, then for someone who can't.

Ask Yourself This...
What small miracle can I acknowledge today that brings me closer to gratitude and presence?

⸸ February 18

Boundaries are important.

Not Today
Sorry...
I'd love to but...
I really wish I could...
Thank you for thinking of me, but...
Thanks for the opportunity, however..
I just can't right now.

You can say "No".
It's allowed.
It's Ok.
It's not a big deal.
It's just a "No".

Boundaries are important.
They protect your time, mind, and heart.
But most importantly, can keep you on your path
when a "Yes" would surely knock you off.

So please,
Just. Say. No.

Ask Yourself This...
How can I embrace the power of "No" to strengthen my boundaries and protect my well-being?

⸸ February 19

Every. Single. Bit.

You're Worthy
You're worthy of friendship
Love
Peace
Warmth
And every blessing that comes your way.
All of it.
Every. Single. Bit.

I just thought I'd remind you.
In case you somehow forgot.

Ask Yourself This...
What small steps can I take today to remind me of my worth and invite love and blessings into my life?

⸸ February 20

An essential part of life.

You are a Gift
You have no idea how much of a gift you are or the impact you make. You can't fully grasp what you mean and how your existence makes the world a better place.

So please, just trust me on this: You're an essential part of life, including mine, simply for having read this.

Ask Yourself This...
How will I begin to truly appreciate the importance of my life and the positive impact I have on others for simply being me?

⸸ February 21

Always Calm, Centered, and Still.

The Eye

See yourself as the Eye of the Storm—
keenly aware of the chaos around you,
but always calm, centered, and still;
Moving slowly and consistently forward,
until the storm disappears.

Ask Yourself This…

What small things can I be sure to do everyday to protect my energy and keep me calm in the face of the storms I encounter?

⸸ February 22

Call It Whatever You Want, But Listen To It.

Forcing the Issue
If it doesn't "feel right,"
Trust that.

If you are doing something because you feel you "should,"
Stop that.

If you're staying in something because you're "scared,"
Leave that.

You have An Inner Guidance System—
Call it your heart.
Call it your gut.
Call it whatever you want, but listen to it,
act on it,and above all, respect it.

Because that feeling deep inside you,
Is never wrong.

Ask Yourself This...
How will I show daily respect for my inner voice by acting on what it's telling me, even when dealing with outside pressures?

February 23

Do not hit the brakes, and try to keep the steering wheel straight.

Black Ice

If you're someone who's never experienced it, Black Ice is transparent, and takes on the color of the surface of the road it's on. It's impossible to see, so one second you're cruising along listening to music, the next, careening seemingly out of control towards disaster.

Kind of like the “Black Ice” we experience in our lives.
The things that we never see coming, that take us from feeling in control and confident, to suddenly being out of control, in danger, and full of fear.

Interestingly enough, here's the advice the US Forest Service gives when you encounter Black Ice:
"If you do hit black ice, your first reaction must be to remain calm and avoid overreacting. The general rule is to do as little as possible and allow the car to pass over the ice. Do not hit the brakes, and try to keep the steering wheel straight."

Turns out to be pretty solid life advice as well...
- Remain calm
- Avoid overreacting
- Release your sense of control
- Keep going
- Try your best to stay on course

***Bonus Advice in Both Cases: PRAY.**

Ask Yourself This...

How can I remind myself to release my need for control when life’s unexpected challenges arise?

⸸ February 24

And I look at you and wonder.

Your Story
I want to know your story.
I want to understand how you came to be here
in this moment, just as you are, with me.

Because I know so little about you, and it's obvious that there's so much more than meets the eye.

I can see it in your eyes—
All those dreams you've had, the struggles, laughter, and tears.
And all the dreams that came true (and especially the ones that didn't).
All part of the person I see smiling for the camera, putting their best foot forward, and trying to fit into a world with ever changing rules and expectations.

The one feeling overwhelmed by it all,
but still standing, still trying, and still smiling—
all the while holding your own (and some for others too).

And I look at you and wonder, if we had the time to sit over a cup of tea on a Sunday afternoon, what stories would you tell?

Ask Yourself This...
What experiences shape who I am and keep me going, and how will I stay true to myself in a changing world?

February 25

I know, there are still horrible things happening in the world.

Did God Stop Talking to Us?

Yesterday I saw four posts in a row from different people in different parts of the world, all talking about God.
One posed the question, "Has God stopped talking to us".
The thought centered on the fact that since the writing of the Bible, nobody has really believed anyone that has said, "God told me".

So the question is why?
Why don't we feel it possible for God to directly communicate with us?
Why, when someone says they got it straight from the Almighty,
do the majority nod and think "Hmmm, ok, suuure you did!"

I believe that God not only hasn't stopped talking to us, but has been nothing short of a chatterbox lately.

I say that because I see an ever increasing openness in people.
A willingness to talk about their spirituality, religion, faith, and beliefs and more importantly, in a very personal and non-judgmental way.

Maybe it's just me, but it seems that God is more present in more lives, in more obvious ways than ever, and I think that the more we're open to loving, listening, and sharing, the more we'll see, hear, and experience all that God wants for us.

Ask Yourself This...

How does this perspective of God speaking to us through our own actions and words feel to me? Does it ring true?

⸸ February 26

You're actually looking in a mirror.

All of Us

Every human has struggled, been in pain and felt insignificant.
Experienced joy, happiness, tragedy, and loss.
And has looked to the sky and wondered what the meaning of it all is.

This humanness—
this shared struggle and wonder,
is what connects the CEO in New York
to the indigenous warrior in the bush.
It's what connects you to me, us to them,
and all of us together.

And while the ways and at what levels
we experience these things are indeed very different,
the effects on us are all the same.

Yes, deep down, in our humanness,
we are all the same.

So when you feel alone
or different, less than, elated, or even joyous,
just remember that somewhere— no, *everywhere*—
people are experiencing the same exact thing as you are.
And that while you think you're looking at strangers,
you're actually looking in a mirror.

Ask Yourself This...

How can I be kind to myself and others in simple ways, knowing we all share similar joys, sorrows, and struggles?

⸸ February 27

You probably need it more than you realize.

Breathing
We act as if breathing is just something we're doing while we're living life, when actually, living life is just something we do while we're breathing.

Take a moment and take a breath—
a real, deep, intentional breath.
Not only do you deserve it,
you need it more than you realize.

Ask Yourself This...
How often do I stop and appreciate the simple act of breathing, recognizing the life it gives me, and how can I do it more?

⸸ February 28

One small action. Today.

Ok, Enough
Right now you're probably experiencing lots of stress and aggravation. You'd love for it to stop, but have determined that the levels of each don't rise quite high enough to expend the time and energy (or really just put up with the BS) that it would take to eliminate them.

So you're making up excuses, justifying inaction, and accepting all of them as just "part of life".

You deserve better. So let's stop that today.

Let's say today is the day where you stop accepting all the crap you've been letting hold you back.
Today is the day that you take *just one small step* toward a solution.
Today is the day you're *done* accepting the low-level hum of stress, pain, and annoyance that's keeping you in a perpetual state of "Grrrr...."

So make that phone call.
Put that terrible food down.
Don't have that drink.
Have that awkward conversation.
Clean out that cabinet.
Go to the gym (or at least dust off the treadmill).
And tell that person you Love them (do that one every day).
One small action.
Today.
Let's go.

Ask Yourself This…
What specific things in my life cause the Grrr…, and what I will do now to start fixing them?

⸸ February 29 *A Bonus Leap Thought!*

Be Wicked Kind Today...
(It's a New England thing)

⸸ March 1

Approach the day with the intent to Love, Listen, and Learn.

Life is Counterintuitive
When all of your effort, stress, worry, and 14-hour workdays don't deliver the results, happiness, or connection you're striving so hard to attain, consider this:

- Giving brings more joy than receiving.
- Rest recharges your energy more than constant pushing ever will.
- Meditation, not obsession, enhances focus.
- Vulnerability is true strength.
- The most powerful words humans can speak are, "Help me."

So Stop.
Breathe.
Relax.

Let go of your expectations and your need for control.
Take in the present moment and the people around you.
Approach each day with the intention to love, listen, and learn.

That pause in your outward effort will bring you more than you ever thought possible.

Promise.

Ask Yourself This...
What part of my life feels out of control, and how can I release my grip to allow growth, peace, or new opportunities to enter?

March 2

It's OK to be "Not OK"...

"I've Been Better…"

I noticed lately that when I'm asked, "How Are You?" the meaning of my responses looks something like this…
Awesome = Really Good
Great = Good
"Good"= "Ok" or "Not good, but I don't want to say it."

I'll be honest—I'm not always awesome, great, or even good.
Sometimes I'm down, struggling, or just plain "Can't Even."
So now when people say, "How are you?" I'm trying to be honest.
If I'm not doing great, I've simply started saying,
"Been better, been worse" or "been better, but ok.".

I've decided to be honest, because just maybe, through my honesty,
Someone else might feel that it's ok to say they're not ok.
And that could really end up meaning something.

So maybe the next time you're not ok, just say it.
We all need to realize that everyone isn't great all the time.
And that it's ok to be "Not ok"…

Ask Yourself This...

What good things might come from being honest about how I'm feeling, and can I commit to it?

⸸ March 3

Once you start down this path, it's impossible to stop.

Finding Your Life Purpose in 4 "Easy" Steps…
I've determined it comes down to doing five things.

1. What's Worth It?
Look back on your life and figure out why you did or didn't stay in those jobs, relationships, or situations. We all make choices to stick around when things get tough or leave when they get uncomfortable. Reflect on that, and you'll find ***what's worth the effort*** to you.

2. Energy
Look way back and think about the times you felt your best, did your best, and achieved things you're most proud of. During those times, what things or people left you feeling inspired and full of possibility? The answers to ***what lights you up*** are there.

3. Forget the Money
Let go of the belief that your life purpose has to be tied to making money, and focus on the times you're in that effortless flow and time disappears; That's where life's magic happens. Do what you love, and the money will follow. Above all, find ***what makes you happy.***

4. Meditate on It
Now ***take a few deep breaths, clear your mind, and wonder about it***. This will probably take a lot of time, but you'll find answers here.

5. Take Action!
When the answer comes, ***unapologetically reach out to those people, do those things, and move in that direction everyday.*** Once you start down this path, you won't want to stop.

Ask Yourself This…
When will I do this practice?

March 4

Today I'm alive.

Not that exciting right?
Today I woke up, talked to my wife for a bit and turned on the heat to get the chill out of the house, then I made a piece of toast and some coffee.

Not that exciting, right?
But what if I told you this instead…

Today I'm alive, breathing, and healthy.
I have love in my life
I have a warm and safe home to live in
I have plenty of food to eat
and I have coffee.

Sounds amazing, right?

So today —
May your mind be present.
Your heart be grateful.
And your coffee, absolutely amazing.

So please go appreciate the day, and all it brings.

Ask Yourself This…
What everyday moments am I taking for granted that, with a shift in perspective, could fill me with appreciation and joy?

⸸ March 5

I have faith in you.

If Nobody Else Tells You Today
You are enough.
I have faith in you.
You are loved.
And most importantly,
it's going to be ok.
Really, it is.

So please don't stop —
Keep going.
Keep trying.
And keep moving.
Because we need you,
more than you'll ever know

Ask Yourself This...
When was the last time I reminded myself that I am enough, and how can I show up for myself today despite any doubts?

⸸ March 6

A child will never ask you to explain why you lost your temper. That's up to you.

Watch Your Temper
We all have moments when we lose our temper with our kids.
It happens.
What matters most is how we handle it afterward.

Taking the time to explain why we got upset as soon as possible is crucial because if we don't, their young minds may create their own distorted version of events—and that story could stay with them for life.

So remember, a child will never ask you to explain why you lost your temper. That's up to you.

Ask Yourself This...
How can I become more aware of my emotional triggers and better manage them, especially with children?

⸸ March 7

Now wouldn't that be an amazing thing?

Your World Kindness Day
World Kindness Day began in 1998 to bridge divides between race, religion, geography, gender, politics, and more.

It's a beautiful thought, and I absolutely love it!
But to make it truly meaningful in our everyday lives,
I have an idea…

Since "*the world*" is such a vast place, why not bring it closer to home and call it "***Your World Kindness Day***"?

Who in *your* world can you give a smile to, hold the door for, be less judgmental toward, or simply choose not to react negatively to? Who can you uplift, make amends with, or help "just because"?

Take a moment to reflect: Who are those people in your life, and what small act of kindness can you offer them today? And even if you can't do it today, simply bringing them to mind is an act of kindness, right?

World Kindness Day can either be a fleeting, idealistic prompt that gets lost in the hustle, or it can be the beginning of *Your World Kindness Week*, *Your World Kindness Month*, or even *Your World Kindness Year*.

Now wouldn't that be amazing?

Ask Yourself This...
Who in my world can I show kindness to today, and what simple action can I take to make a difference in their life?

⸸ March 8

If you read nothing else in this book, read this.

The Storm of Life

Just after midnight on **March 8th, 2020**, I was heading to bed when, out of nowhere, I felt the need to go back down to our finished basement. I went down and just stood there, feeling confused because I had no reason to be there. After a confusing minute or two, I decided to head back up to bed.

As I passed by my journal on the table, I thought that maybe I should sit down and write. I checked my phone; it was 12:12 a.m. I started writing, just reflections on the day, feeling tired. Nothing meaningful really. It felt like one of those moments where you're just going through the motions. So I decided to stop.

Then, for some reason, I made a ***bold vertical line*** after the last word I'd written. I never do that. And right after, I felt—maybe even heard—something say, "*Don't think, just write this.*"

For context, my writing process has always been pretty straightforward. I usually have one line pop into my head, then I'll write for 10-15 minutes, editing as I go. Each "Thought" takes anywhere from 10 to 25 minutes to complete.

But this one? I don't remember writing the specifics at all.

I wrote it in less than two minutes, not thinking about a single word or pausing for even a fraction of a second. When I finished, I just knew to stop and made another bold vertical line, just like before.

Here it is—exactly as I wrote it. No edits, no revisions.

"Don't judge the things you see, feel or hear.
Don't try to understand the meaning of the existence you have.
I am here.
I am always here.
I listen. I know. I am.
The only thing you must do is nothing.
I am in control of it all.
I know better than you what you must do, where you must be, and what you must say.
Trust me.
Trust me with your life, your spirit, your soul.
Because your soul was created by me, came from me,
IS ME.
Your soul. Your beautiful soul. The only creation you have. The only creation you need.
Come to me then.
Lay down what you have.
Your burdens, your pain, your madness.
Show them to me in the light of day.
Show them to me. Do not hide, do not run, be afraid, or wither like a branch on a dying tree.
Speak.
Speak your truth and be healed.
For I am the one. I am the master.
I created all, everything you see, feel, hear, and touch - is me. Be still.
Let me comfort you.
Let me Love you.
Let me take you from this into my arms and shoulder your burden.
You are my child.
The one I look after, see beyond for, and understand.
So be still in this storm that I also created.
That I also control.
That I also own.
This storm. A storm of lessons in the night.
This storm of goodness and light.
This storm that will make you the one you are supposed to be.
This storm of being.
This storm of Life."

⸸ March 9

...gently acknowledge the need for change.

Cleansing

That accumulated soot of life.
The lies you've always told yourself about how others perceive you.
The nagging feeling that you've missed important lessons along the way.
The self-limitations and weight of resentment, regret, envy, and lack.

All those layers, built up over so many years, conversations, "failures," effort, circumstances, and yes, even uncontrollable fate.

Stop now for a moment and visualize it. You, trying to look through all that, while at the same time trying to be seen by those on the other side.
How frustrating.
How sad.
How unnecessary.

Take a breath now, and think about what those layers are,
how long they've been there,
and how used to them you've become.
Why you've just accepted that
"That's just the way it is" and "That's just how I am."

Please don't accept that anymore.
You've done the very best you can
and made it this far,
so see the soot for what it really is,
and start wiping it clean.

Ask Yourself This...

What emotional baggage or limiting beliefs have been blocking my growth, and how will I begin letting them go?

⸸ March 10

Consistency is the key to making everything worth it possible.
So work on your dream every day.
Even if it's just a minute.

You've got this.

March 11

...every minute has a purpose.

God Smiled, and You Were Born
You were born with a purpose—
something *only you* were meant to do.

So regardless of what has happened in the past, what expectations haven't been met, or how seemingly mundane your days seem to be, every minute has been a part of the grand plan for your life.

Because you were born, life has been better for more people than you could ever imagine. Some in simple, fleeting ways, and others who, without you, would be in a far worse place.

And even though it is impossible to see the positive impact you continue to make on the world, please trust that it's true,
and because of it, God continues to smile.

Ask Yourself This...
What is one way I can become more aware of how my actions contribute to making the world better, fully accepting my purpose?

⸸ March 12

Take a deep breath.

Quick Reminder
Stop right now.
Take a deep breath.
Drop your shoulders.
Release the tension in your stomach.
No, really—do this right now. I know you need it.
(That's all for today, but it's more than enough if you remember to keep doing it.)

Ask Yourself This...
How will I stay mindful and take breaks for relaxation and self-care throughout the day?

March 13

...trust your mind and live in fear.

Life is Simple; It's You That's Complicated

Life is, and always will be, what you make it.
So you have a choice:
Either trust your *heart* and embrace the process of life—
accepting that it will continuously come together and fall apart while looking for the lessons along the way. Or, trust your *mind*, live in fear, trying to predict what will be while attempting to control the process.

The first is simple but can feel impossibly hard.
The second is maddening, stressful, and well, just impossible.
I say trust your heart.
It will never let you down.

Ask Yourself This...

How do I remind myself to trust my heart and go with life's flow, even in challenging times?

March 14

You can make someone's life better right now.

If you can say or do anything to make someone happy right now, do that.
Kindness is simple, quick, and doesn't have to cost anything.
Kindness can be a smile, a thought, or simply a word.
Yes, you can make someone's life better right now.
by simply thinking of them and sending good energy their way.
So, who will you be kind to today?

Ask Yourself This...
How can I make bringing happiness to others a habit, and how can I incorporate it into my everyday life?

March 15

...why then don't we just eat all the damned vegetables?

All the Advice Has Been Given
It seems that all the life advice we'll ever need has been given,
We've had the keys to living our "Best Life" for decades.

So why then don't we just eat the vegetables, work out daily, meditate, put the phones down, forgive, love, be authentic, pray, be selfless, get more sleep, let things go, and well, just *breathe* correctly?

It's because our desire for comfort is even more powerful than our need for anything other than our basic safety. And that's why we stay in our comfort zones rather than doing the hard work to improve.

The key to growth then isn't to step *out of* your comfort zone, but to *expand it* by consistently taking tiny steps in the right direction.
So tiny, in fact, that they go virtually unnoticed by your internal comfort police, but over time are significant enough to build an entirely new life.

So get to work, you have a comfort zone to expand!

Ask Yourself This...
What is one small, actionable step I can take today that will expand my comfort zone and help me grow?

⸸ March 16

So what are you missing?

How many dreams have died because they didn't make financial sense?
When I opened BeanTowne Coffee House, I saw it as a place that would have live music, events, and other fun stuff.
But once the actual planning of these things started,
they turned into work, staffing, cleanup, and extra prep.
At the end of the day, they just didn't seem "worth it".

But I was missing the point all these years.
The events aren't about money, they're about fun and having people in the community connect with each other.

The interesting thing is once I looked at it from this perspective,
everything changed, and it all seemed more than "worth it".

So what is that dream that you've decided isn't "worth it",
and more importantly, why?

Ask Yourself This...
What dreams or passions did I put aside because of money, and how will I find joy in them again?

March 17

How we define success to our children will surely determine the future of the world.

Think about that.

Ask Yourself This...
How do I show kids that success is more than just money and status, and instead focus on things like empathy, kindness, and positive impact?

March 18

... a constantly moving target is almost impossible to hit.

Moving Targets

You go through life feeling that you're always on the journey
But never at the destination. Always seeking and rarely finding—
"almost there" but never feeling you've made it.
And the reason is simple: A constantly moving target is almost impossible to hit.

The fact is your life is in a state of constant evolution, but you keep making plans and setting goals like your situation will stay exactly the same.

But life doesn't work like that.

Whether you like it or not, life takes all of your best intentions— your energy, drive, and aspirations— and directs them to a place, time, and configuration that will serve you best.

So yes, make those plans, set those goals, and pour love into those relationships. But once you do, accept them as nothing more than your intent at that particular moment. Continue to pour your love and energy into making them happen, but never forget that life will always do its thing— and it will always be for the best.

Ask Yourself This...

How will I practice letting go of expectations and embracing the unpredictability of life?

⸸ March 19

Making sense of the senseless and securing your place in the world.

Mental Health

Don't confuse mental strength with mental health.
Mental strength is resilience, grit, and the ability to navigate what life throws at you. It's what you lean on when the chips are down and there's nobody to rely on but yourself.

Mental health, on the other hand, is different—
it's wider and deeper.

It encompasses everything about you, helping make sense of the senseless, and is the foundation upon which your life will be built.

So yes, having mental strength is important,
but mental health is truly what you need to understand
what you need to be so strong for in the first place.

Ask Yourself This…

What will I do today to prioritize my mental health?

⸸ March 20

You matter...

PSST.....
I believe in you...
You can do it...
You have great ideas...
There's nobody else like you...
The world needs you just like you are...
You're smart..
You matter...
You're strong...
You are loved...
This is all true.
Please believe this.
Now pass it on to someone who needs to hear it too…

Ask Yourself This...
How did this thought make me feel, and what does that say about my sense of self?

March 21

My contact info is in the back.

Connecting
If you're a person who wants to spread as much positivity, joy, and inspiration as they possibly can in this life,
I want to connect with you.
This has nothing to do with business, money, or "opportunities", and everything to do with the fact that like-minded people need to know and learn from each other.
My contact info is below.
Drop me a line!

Ask Yourself This…
Is there any reason why I shouldn't pop Ed an email at Ed@thoughtuary.com?

⸸ March 22

I hope you feel loved today.
That's all.

March 23

You deserve the feeling.

Reality Check
Today, I hope you see yourself as the people who love you do—
not just how you think they see you, but how they truly see you.
You deserve that feeling.
So please, take a moment now and think about this:
How do they see you, truly, in their hearts?

Ask Yourself This...
What is one way I can embody the love and appreciation others have for me today?

March 24

Others Expectations Are Not Your Responsibilities.
And of Course, Vice Versa.

Ask Yourself This…

How often do I put other people's expectations above my own wants and needs, and on the flip side, do I have a tendency to expect people to prioritize mine over theirs?

⸸ March 25

You deserve *all the fun*.

The Most Important Question
"What's the absolute most fun thing I could do today?"
Ask this question, then, try to do at least a version of it.

Make it attainable, and protect your answer against all the practical "buts" your mind will immediately throw at you like:
"I don't have time,"
"I should be more productive,"
or "It's not important."

You deserve *all the fun.*
So please, ask yourself this question often—
then go and make it happen.

Ask Yourself This…
Why don't I prioritize fun in my life more often, and isn't it about time I did?

⸸ March 26

That voice in your head is wrong.
It definitely wasn't a big deal.
Probably nobody noticed,
and even if they did,
they've already forgotten about it.
You probably should too...

Ask Yourself This...
Isn't it about time I accepted the fact that everyone isn't analyzing everything I do or say?

March 27

Without failure, we learn nothing.

Failing Miserably
You're probably going to fail at something today—that's just a fact of life.
But how you react to that failure is crucial.

You could choose to be miserable, frustrated, and beat yourself up, or you could embrace that failure as a seed of future success, and keep moving forward.

Without our failures, we learn nothing, build no resilience, and lack perspective. So whatever failure comes your way today, take it in stride, and see it for the growth opportunity it really is.

Ask Yourself This...
What lesson is my failure teaching me that I couldn't have learned any other way?

⸸ March 28

You're not failing.

Falling Behind
Sometimes the one who falls behind the pack simply becomes the leader of their own life.
That took me decades to realize.

Ask Yourself This…
When will I finally release external expectations, stop comparing myself to others, and fully embrace that I am prepared to lead?

March 29

We mind-meld at the worst possible times.

Mind-Melding and the Dark Side of Empathy
It's easy to get sucked into another's energy, priorities, and emotions, especially when someone you love is going through a hard time.

Unfortunately, our good intentions and desire (no, need) for everything to be ok often pull us into their vortex of confusion, pain, doubt, and negativity.

We tend to mind-meld at the worst possible times.
It's the dark side of empathy.

The goal is to walk beside them, not to feel their pain so deeply that it truly becomes your own.

It's hard to "rise above" in this way, but it's the most important thing you can do when someone you love is walking a hard road.

So create that lane of support next to them and stay in it as long as they need—but remember to *always* protect your own emotional well-being.

Ask Yourself This…
Do I tend to take on others' pain, doubt, and negativity? And what can I do to stop?

March 30

...Love will always find the right words.

Speak from Your Heart

Always speak to the people who matter most as if you love them more than anything in the world—especially when you feel they don't deserve it. Because Love has a way of always finding the right words to heal, uplift, and inspire change, even when it feels the hardest.

When you need it most, tapping into the deepest part of your love and speaking directly from your heart can heal and strengthen bonds in ways nothing else can.

You just need to be present enough, to give it a chance.

Ask Yourself This...

How can I make speaking from a place of love a habit, even during disagreements or tough emotions?

March 31

...real growth is all but inevitable.

Vulnerability = Strength

Vulnerability leads to openness.
Openness leads to honesty.
Honesty leads to communication.
Communication leads to connection.
Connection leads to community.
And community? It's not just where problems get solved more quickly, but where real progress, genuine change, and significant growth become inevitable.

Yes, vulnerability is strength—and so much more.

Ask Yourself This...

How does embracing my vulnerability open the door to deeper connections with others?

⸸ April 1

You'll get to see other human beings light up.

Eye Contact

Try This.

Tomorrow, try to make eye contact and smile as much as possible. You'll get to see other human beings light up—even if just for a moment—because of something you did. And that always makes for a really great day.

Ask Yourself This...

What steps can I take to create more genuine and warm interactions into my daily life?

April 2

Give us your good enough.

Perfect Things...
How many perfect things have died in people's minds, when the "good enough" version would have surely changed the world?
So please don't wait.
Give us your good enough, and we'll help you make it perfect.

Ask Yourself This...
How has perfectionism held me back from sharing my ideas or creations in the past, and what will I do to change it?

♆ April 3

... I also learned I have a lot to learn.

What I Learned from Spending Three Days with 1,000 Women
I once spoke at a NAWBO Conference, they exist to support women entrepreneurs. As the only male speaker, I had the rare opportunity to be immersed in the culture of women for three days. Here's what I learned.

First, Sisterhood.
These women care for, support, and truly listen to each other. Their egoless interactions and the way they *gently* pushed each other really moved me.

Second, Drive.
"If there isn't a seat at the table, build your own table." Now I've been attending conferences for decades, but this was different. It was one voice made up of 1,000, all going in the same direction with an intense, focused energy.

Third, Empathy and Heart.
They get that an empathetic and heart-based business isn't weak but dynamically strong. And being vulnerable enough to admit that you *don't know* is the best leadership advice you could give or receive.

Fourth, Fun.
They had fun, were silly, and laughed. There was lightness and positivity everywhere. While they were there on business, they didn't take themselves too seriously, which seemed to be the foundation of the entire experience.

I was happy to see a lot of what I have based my businesses on present here, *but I also learned I have a lot to learn*, and I think maybe it's time for men to look, listen, and take some notes.

Ask Yourself This... Where can I find new experiences to expand my understanding and challenge my assumptions?

⸸ April 4

...find your thing and make it happen.

No Human is Limited
I just read about a guy that ran a marathon in under two hours. That's right, a pace of 4.5-minute miles for 26 miles.

Damn.

Now, we can look at this and think, "I could never do that", or even see it as proof that our own lives are less meaningful, uninspired, or even boring by comparison. Or, we could look at this guy as proof that dreams can actually come true. That by using OUR OWN innate talents, we too can make it to the pinnacle and do our own version of running like lightning for 2 hours straight.

Let's be honest, chances are slim to none that any of us will ever break a world record or rise to international fame, but ALL of us are born with something in us that is more valuable than all the medals in the world, and that is the ability to fulfill what we are ACTUALLY HERE TO DO. Now the fact is that you're much more similar to this guy than not (it's true).

So find your thing and make it happen. That guy did, and so can you. Oh, and that guy's name is Eliud Kipchoge!

Ask Yourself This...
What steps will I take right now to align my actions with my true purpose?

⸸ April 5

Focus on making the best of your moments, and your life will take care of itself.

Ask Yourself This...
How will I shift my focus to stay in the now and simply be content with the journey, and what resources are out there to help me make it happen?

April 6

It all starts at this very moment.

Just a Little...
If we all poured just a *little* more love and kindness into the world,
a massive positive shift would unfold in all our lives.
Just.
A little.
More.
So go into the day expecting something good to happen,
then do something good yourself.
It all starts at this very moment,
with you.

Ask Yourself This...
What is one simple way I will create a mindset of positivity and expect good things to happen?

April 7

...shed what no longer fits and embrace the real you.

Do You Remember?
Do you remember who you were before the world told you who you should be? The one before the expectations, labels, and outside voices shaped who you are now?

Well even if you don't, it's not too late to reconnect, shed what no longer fits, and embrace the real you.

Because I promise you, the person untouched by the world
is still inside, just waiting.

Ask Yourself This...
What is one way I can begin to rediscover the "real me," and what positive things could come from it?

April 8

I was simply wandering.

All who wander aren't lost, but all who are lost aren't wanderers...
Today I took a ride with no planned destination. Though I had no clue where I was (somewhere in Maine), I wasn't lost. I was simply wandering, excited to see what wonderful thing might be around the corner.

And you know what? I found several—
ones I probably would've driven right by if I hadn't simply been wandering without expectation.

Did you ever notice that life works the same way?
That we tend to find more love, treasure, wonder, and joy when we aren't looking for it?

So I hope the next time you find yourself with your head down,
trying your hardest to make something happen
You'll think of my little trip to Maine
and simply wander.

Ask Yourself This...
What is one way I can remind myself to wander, and more importantly, how can I shift my mindset to allow myself to?

April 9

Once I made that mindset shift, it has become almost automatic.

Looking for Similarities & Scratching the Surface
During my aimless wandering yesterday, I serendipitously came upon a cool little shop. I noticed a "50% off the entire store" sign on a table and was curious why there was such a little sign for such a big announcement.

So I started talking to the owner, who confirmed she was closing the store after seven years. Then I did something I often do that has led to so many great connections and conversations—
I found a similarity, then scratched the surface.

I shared that I too had just closed a store and asked, "Is your moving on a good thing or a not-so-good thing?" That question led to a wonderful conversation in which she shared her desire to move to Austin, Texas, to start over after having some troubles.

I left not only with some cool gifts for my family but, more importantly, a new friend and a great memory. (I'll add that most times, finding that similarity isn't that easy. It takes observation and a willingness to see yourself in others—which is definitely a practice.)

So the next time you see something that makes you wonder, instead of letting it pass as a fleeting moment, pause and get curious—overcome the feeling of awkwardness you'll most likely feel then find a similarity or simply scratch the surface.

There you will find the stuff that makes life truly interesting.

Ask Yourself This…
How can I shift my mindset to one of curiosity in my everyday life?

April 10

...rockets don't go straight up forever.

Leveling Out

When you level up, you also have to level out.
Find that new normal and move in.
Because rockets don't go straight up forever—
eventually, they stop pushing through boundaries,
turn off their jets, and find their orbit.

So breathe, relax, sleep, and have gratitude.
Then refuel your rockets, and start to wonder all over again.

Ask Yourself This...

During periods of growth, do I tend to pause, refuel, and reflect? Or do I push without recognizing my new normal - and why?

⸸ April 11

You need more sleep. Seriously.

Ask Yourself This...
What are some ways I can improve my sleep quality and ensure I *consistently* get the rest I need?

April 12

You were born perfectly suited.

What are you waiting for?
You were born perfectly suited and fully prepared for what you are destined to do, which most likely has *little to nothing* to do with your current job title.

So isn't it time you did something about it?

Ask Yourself This...
What bold step **will** I take today to align my life with my true calling?

⸸ April 13

Say it more often, and your life will get better.

Help
Why is it that we have no problem seeking immediate help when we have a problem with a tech issue, but almost never do when we have a problem with life?

The most powerful sentence a human being can say is "I need help" Say it more often, and your life will get better.

Promise.

Ask Yourself This...
How will I start to get comfortable asking for more help?

⸸ April 14

...you've handled more than this before.

You've Got This
You have a lot coming at you right now,
and I know at times it must seem overwhelming—
But I know you've handled more than this before—*a lot more.*

So much so that, most likely, what you're going through right now pales in comparison to everything you've overcome in the past.
And deep down, you know it.

Yet, when challenges arise, it's almost impossible not to focus on the pain of the sudden shift from "normal", and not on the realization that what challenges you now probably doesn't rise to the level of the worst thing you've already proven you can get through.

I know that in this moment, gaining that perspective requires you to step back and look at the big picture exactly when the force sucking you into your problems is at its greatest—and this can seem impossible.

Which is why I wrote this for you—
To give you this moment to realize the power of your PROVEN strength, resilience, perseverance, and grit has already gotten you through everything life's thrown at you up to this moment, just as it will now.

You've got this, just like you always have.

Ask Yourself This...
When will I finally accept that my life has prepared me for the challenges I now face, even though it doesn't feel like it?

⸸ April 15

Expect it.

The Rhythm of Life
Your life has never been wonderful or terrible forever.
Things continuously come together and fall apart, but somehow you're always surprised when they do.

Yes, change is inevitable.

So accept and love the journey to the peaks,
but be prepared for the dips to the valleys below—
because you'll experience all of it not only in a lifetime,
but every. single. day.

Expect it.

Ask Yourself This...
What is one way I can prepare myself mentally and emotionally for the ups and downs that life brings?

⸸ April 16

It takes just a few seconds.

Great job!
The moment you think, "That person's doing a great job," is the moment you should tell them. It takes just a few seconds, but seriously, don't we all need a bit of "You're Awesome" now and then?

And, if nobody else has told you today, I think you're doing a great job, and the world is better because you're in it!

Ask Yourself This…
Who can I recognize today for their hard work or kindness, and how will I show my appreciation to them?

⸸ April 17

...let them know they're not just a cog in the machinery of our day.

The Few Extra Words

I was at Walgreens. The cashier was doing her best.
Smiling at unsmiling people.
Asking for rewards numbers and wishing good days.
Three people in a row barely said a word.
Three people in a row missed the opportunity to make one of those three-second connections that makes life just a little bit brighter.

So I returned her smile, made a joke, and we shared a laugh.
Before I left the counter, I said, "You're very pleasant; I hope you have a good rest of your day." I saw her shoulders drop and smile widened as she said, "Thank you! You too!"

"You're very pleasant."
A small compliment that said so much more.
Three words that proved someone not only saw her as a person, but also recognized how hard she was trying.
Three words that said, to at least one person, "Your smile did make a difference."

Yes, this was just a simple interaction.
One of a thousand moments we all share with others every day.
But it was also one of a thousand opportunities we have to say just those few extra words to let them know they're relevant
and not just a cog in the machinery of our day.

Those few words can also turn a mundane interaction into one you remember four days later, just like I am now.

Ask Yourself This...

How will I uplift and validate the people I see throughout my day?

⸸ April 18

...please get some rest today.

R.E.S.T.
Replenish Energy with Silence & Time

I'm pretty sure you could use some more sleep,
but I'm absolutely certain you need more R.E.S.T..
Just some time in silence to breathe, let your brain decompress, and reset. So please get some rest today.
You need it.

Ask Yourself This…
How will I create space in my daily routine for intentional R.E.S.T.?

⸸ April 19

...negativity comes like a drop of oil on water.

Oil & Water

Watch a group of five-year-olds playing, and you'll quickly see it's our inherent nature to be joyous, curious, accepting, and free. But at some point, negativity creeps in, spreading like a drop of oil on water, until it covers almost all that was once so pure. It seems we then spend the rest of our lives slowly cleaning up that mess.

So be mindful of those drops—
the ones that come your way and the ones you spread yourself, especially around kids. Because their natural joy (and protecting it) is needed now more than ever.

Ask Yourself This...

How can I become more aware of the exact moments when negativity enters my life and affects my perspective?

⸸ April 20

At this very moment.

Your Power
Please understand that regardless of your state of mind, physical condition, or emotional well-being, you are just as capable as the most influential speaker on the planet of making a difference in someone's life—right here and right now.

At this very moment, you can help uplift someone, forward their journey, or simply make them feel heard, acknowledged, and seen.

If you're not near anyone right now, take a moment to go online and send a message to some of your friends letting them know how much they mean to you, or acknowledging them for something they've said or done. This could not only make all the difference in their day, but also just might be needed in that moment more than you could ever imagine.

Ask Yourself This…
How can I become more aware of the opportunities around me to make a positive difference in someone's life?

⸸ April 21

...you're building resilience with every step.

The Path of Resilience

The hard times that are now just distant memories were once the things that paralyzed you with fear, and shook you to the core.
Yet they're also the struggles you got through, overcame,
and emerged from wiser, tougher, and better prepared for whatever you're facing now.

So as you're looking for a path out of this darkness, just know that you're building resilience with every step. And that sometime in the future, what you learned during this time will get you through whatever comes next.

But for now—
Drop your expectation
Release your sense of control
Breathe
Love yourself
And be as strong as you have to for as long as it takes.

You'll get through this darkness just as you have every time before.
Because light *always* finds a way.

Ask Yourself This...

How will I remind myself that I am prepared for whatever I am facing, and that light always finds a way?

⸸ April 22

Take a stand.

Apathy
Apathy turns the unacceptable into your new normal.
Take a stand.

Ask Yourself This...
What are the specific things in my life that I find unacceptable, and what will I do to change them?

♆ April 23

This is written for everyone who thinks and feels deeply, but are still keeping it inside...

Inner Thoughts
I care.
I care about people and the world.
I tear up at the oddest moments,
like when I see a mother smile at her child.
I care about how you are what you're going through,
and I want to help.

But I struggle with those unwritten rules
of what to say and when to say it,
when to reach out and when to let go.
And when I want to connect, I worry about being too forward
or about being the only one doing it.

And sometimes I find this paralyzing.

I feel deeply that these are the things that must change—
this ego,
this lack of openness,
this half-honesty.
These barriers keep me from you
and us from everyone else.

So if you feel this way too, please know you're not alone.

Ask Yourself This...
When will I simply accept my open heart as a beautiful thing, and follow it when the urge comes to connect with another?

⸸ April 24

The curious are the ones who move the world.

Stay Curious
Accepting things they way they are is safe
It takes less energy, moves you more quickly through your day,
and keeps things going at a steady, even pace.

But it also limits your ability to grow, is less exciting,
and places a low ceiling over your fun.

Being constantly curious on the other hand is quite the opposite.
New worlds open, possibility is everywhere, and even the seemingly
mundane can turn into a moment you'll remember forever.

So be present, mind your thoughts, and question everything.
The curious are the ones who move the world.
Be curious.

Ask Yourself This…
If I became more curious, how would my life change?

⸸ April 25

Meditation is the New Merlot.

Ask Yourself This…
Isn't it about time I made better choices about how I relax, unwind, and reset? And if I do, what long term benefits will this have?

April 26

Create the crack in the surface that lets love do what love does best.

Let Love Flow
Love is like water.
It finds its way into the smallest places,
filling the cracks and crevices in our lives,
working its way into spots we never knew needed it so much.
It's slow, patient, but also needs to flow.
When stagnant, love becomes a mere reflecting pool—
not the mighty river it's meant to be.

So today, make love possible.

Create the crack in the surface that lets love do what it does best:
heal,
uplift,
calm,
warm,
and complete our souls.

Remember this later today when love wants to flow toward another. But the dam of hesitation rises. Use this thought as your hammer—create the crack, and let love do its thing.

Ask Yourself This…
How will I allow love to break through hesitation and flow more freely into my relationships, my experiences, and my self-care?

⸸ April 27

How many "Likes" equal happiness?

Only One Like

So you're disappointed that the post you thought was going to get a ton of attention only got one like. And you're feeling neglected, ignored, (and yes, maybe even a little angry).

So here's my question:
How many "Likes" equals happiness?
How many "Comments" create fulfillment?
How many "Shares" bring joy?

Think about that for a minute.
If this resonates with you, maybe you should take a break from social media, and start making the effort to connect with friends in person instead.
Isn't it about time?

Ask Yourself This...

How can I shift my mindset to rely less on external validation?

April 28

...when will you start again?

Dance
Watching a child skip across a room is proof that we're meant to be joyous and dance through life.

So when and why did you stop dancing?
Where did that joy go?
And more importantly, how will you get it back?

Ask Yourself This...
What brought me joy in the past, and how can I recapture the feeling of dancing through life?

April 29

The other side of wondering.

It's not for me to know
Sometimes I wonder what the point is—
Why do I get up every day, go out into the world, and do what I do?
What this life is, and why it's a non-stop ride of challenges and joys.
I wonder where I came from—out there, in here, or some otherworldly place? And I wonder what's next, and where I'll go when the time finally comes for me to take my leave?

But for all my wondering
I know that it's not for me to know.
And that I'll never fully understand this life while I'm in this life.

So I simply have faith that there's a point to getting up every day
going out into the world and doing the things I do.
And I lean on it to keep me going when all I want to do is stop.

So my wish for you is that you'll be blessed with the gift of faith
in yourself,
the world,
and yes, that place you'll go, when the time comes for you to take your leave.

Ask Yourself This...
How can I deepen my faith, make it more present in my everyday life, and use it to increase the happiness in my life?

April 30

Perhaps you've just taken the first step on the right path.

Shift
I don't know what it is,
but I get the sense something changed in you.
Something's shifted.
An opening? a light? an awakening?
I'm not sure, but it is something.

Perhaps you've just taken the first step on the right path.
Perhaps you're starting to discover who you really are.
Or maybe it's just that you're finally starting to breathe.

Whatever it is, please explore it.
Because I get the feeling that if you do,
it will truly make all the difference in the world.

Ask Yourself This...
What signs or feelings have I noticed within myself that show a shift towards a deeper understanding of my true self?

⸸ May 1

You don't have to keep hiding.

Beneath the Veil
I know there's a "you" you've kept hidden.
the "you" behind the pictures,
the "you" beneath the veil,
the "you" whose smile is anything but bright.

I see the weight you carry, the unspoken words and untold stories,
the thoughts that linger in the quiet moments,
and the fears you bury deep, hoping no one will notice.

But despite all the things you're not ready to talk about,
the masks you wear, and the walls you've built,
I can tell you this—
You don't have to keep hiding.
We're ready to hear your truth.
I promise.

Ask Yourself This...
Will I allow others to see my true self? If not, why?

⸸ May 2

What kind of wake will you leave today?

What You Leave in Your Wake
We sail headlong into each day—
Braving the headwinds, waves, and rising tides,
moving forward, pushing through, and making ourselves known.
And in doing so leaving a wake in which others might follow to make their journey a little easier to bear.

So what kind of wake will you leave today?
Will it be wide and calm or narrow and choppy?
Will others glide gently through, or be capsized by your turbulence?
That's up to you to decide.

So smile, breathe, and bring a positive attitude into your day,
Then do your very best, to leave a Good Wake.

Ask Yourself This...
What actions will I take to create a calm and expansive wake around me?

May 3

...realize the blessing in the doing.

Exhaustion
Bone tired.
Not sleeping.
Constantly "on".
Figuring.
Solving.
Helping.
Doing.

It never seems to stop, makes you wonder if it's all worth it,
and if you're *really* making a difference.

Well the truth is, that you matter more than you can imagine. Without your constant effort, those you love so deeply would certainly struggle, and the pain of that would certainly outweigh anything you're experiencing now.

So yes you're tired, but please, for the good of us all
Keep going.

Ask Yourself This...
Can I finally acknowledge and appreciate the positive impact I have on those I love? If not, why?

⸸ May 4

Maybe if we started sharing stories of our failures as well as our successes, the world would be a better place.

Ask Yourself This...
What failure have I experienced that taught me a valuable lesson, and how can I share that story to inspire others?

⸸ May 5

Perhaps that line was never defined.

Enough

Perhaps it's because you were never told when "enough" is.
Perhaps you were raised to value accumulation over appreciation.
Perhaps that line was never defined, and now "enough" feels like an unattainable horizon.

Maybe that's why you perceive yourself as living a life of scarcity,
failing to recognize the reality of your almost obscene abundance.

So perhaps it's time to slow down, brew a nice cup of tea,
and realize just how much you truly have.

Ask Yourself This...

What is truly "enough" for me to live a simple, happy life?

⸸ May 6

I'm asking if you've had all the soft and hard conversations you need to have.

Prepare to Die
Uncomfortable, right?
That thought?
Preparing for the day when you will no longer "be" (well, at least here anyway).
So I have to ask:
Are you prepared?
Are your "Affairs" in order?

Now I'm not asking if you've called a lawyer to talk about your will. I'm asking if you've told the people you love how you really feel. I'm asking if you've had all the soft and hard conversations you need to have— the ones where you say things that needed to be said for a long time (or at least more often).

Now odds are that today isn't your last day.
But one day will be.
So wouldn't it be nice when that day does come,
that nothing is left unsaid?

Ask Yourself This...
Am I holding back from expressing my true feelings to the people who mean something to me? If so, why?

⸸ May 7

I believe this is how we're supposed to feel all the time....

First Light
The first moment in the morning,
still drifting between dreams and the day.
Waking from deep sleep, not quite knowing where you are.

That moment before the world rushes in,
before your mind reminds you of worries, problems, and fears.

That one.
When you know you're awake,
yet everything feels perfect.

That moment,
when your mind is quiet, and your soul is in control.
Thoughtless.

I believe this is how we're meant to feel all the time—
Rested and at peace.
Aware but unencumbered.

I guess we can only dream…

Ask Yourself This...
What brings me a sense of tranquility and helps me disconnect from the noise and busyness of life?

⸸ May 8

The Weight of Words

Your Words
Tell a 4-year-old that Santa exists,
and they'll believe it for the rest of their childhood.
Tell them what they lack,
and they'll believe it for the rest of their lives.

Ask Yourself This…
How much do I think about the impact my words have, especially on children? Am I honoring the responsibility that comes with that?

⸸ May 9

You only have so much time and energy.

Shifting Lanes
There are times in life to focus on moving yourself forward—
your career, goals, dreams, and aspirations.
And then there are times to focus on those who need you—their struggles, challenges, or their journeys through sickness, upheaval, or distress.

A truly successful life—one where your energy is directed at what matters most requires not just an awareness of both your needs and the needs of those you love, but also the ability to shift your perspective with ease, depending on what's most important at the moment.

Because the longer it takes to make that shift, the more discontent, anger, and resentment build.

On one side, there's the frustration of feeling unsupported or ignored by those who don't have the capacity to help while you pursue your own dreams.

On the other, there's the feeling of being trapped in service to someone whose time of need may have passed,
while greatness feels just beyond your reach.

The key is being able to make the shift from your needs to theirs and back again without hesitation, because it frees you from the feeling of being in the wrong place, doing the wrong thing, and never enough.

So stay mindful of those around you, and be ready to shift your focus to show up for both yourself and others fully and without regret at a moment's notice.

Ask Yourself This…
How can I catch myself when discontent, anger, and resentment build because I feel I'm in the wrong place, always behind, and never enough?

⸸ May 10

Set the boundary, and set it tight.

Draw the Line
Today I want you to become aware of the noise and negativity that surrounds you, and more importantly, bring into focus what you're letting in. All of these are carefully crafted distractions designed to make you feel, act, and respond a certain way. You know, the ones making your life worse.

So take a day and be mindful of what you see and hear, ask yourself how it all makes you feel, then identify what has to go.

So what noise will you silence?
What negativity will you stop feeding to your heart, mind,
and soul?
Where will you draw the line on things you accept into your life?

Please set the boundary, and set it tight.
Protect yourself like you would a child, because honestly,
The child that you once were is still inside you,
and wants innocence back.

Ask Yourself This…
Isn't it about time I became more aware of the negativity, divisions, violence, and fear-based influences in my life, and recaptured some of the innocence I've lost along the way?

⸸ May 11

Maybe there's something in these words you need to hear.

Why I Write
I write these things for you because maybe our connection isn't accidental, and there's something in these words you need to hear.

I write these things for me, because for too long I ignored this need for expression, the time has come for me to breathe life into the thoughts that run through my mind.

I write these things for us, because maybe in these words and through this connection, we can share a moment each day that leaves us a little more reflective, and a little less on edge, and a little better off…

So thank you for being half of this whole.
Without you, I wouldn't have the inspiration to write these things, and the words you see here would've simply been random thoughts that passed quickly through my mind, never to see the light of day.

Ask Yourself This…
Who can I share some of the thoughts and experiences I've had when reading this book with?

⸸ May 12

The inevitable rise from an almost imperceptible fall.

Cashier
She wants to do her best, this woman here before me
For her family, her friends, and herself.
But it seems "herself" is always last.
"Herself" is always tired.
"Herself" is often ignored…
But she wants to do her best.
So she does, and she does, and she does.
All the while losing herself in the things she knows matter so much, but somehow, it seems, only to her.
Lately though, she's been feeling a shift.
Deep, honest looks in the mirror.
The kind that only happens after you've been stripped bare.
She feels the time is approaching for her to awaken.
To take responsibility for the unacceptable things she's accepted,
And for the lies she convinced herself were true.
She thinks her strength is coming.
That courage is coming.
The inevitable rise from an almost imperceptible fall.
It's coming.
No, it's here.
It's here in the acceptance of the past and gratitude for lessons learned.
It's here in the deep knowing that it was all worth it—
That her selfless dedication to being *in* service to the people and ideals she held dear is not cause for regret, but a celebration of great accomplishment.
Because she didn't do it for thanks, or praise, or acknowledgment.
She did it out of love—a deep and selfless love that only comes from the core of your being.
One she now knows—is proof of a life well lived.
So if you see yourself in her...
If the time has come to look into your own mirror,
and speak your own truth—

Then take a breath, honor the accomplishments of your past,
Find your courage, and by all means—
Rise.

Ask Yourself This…

Have I lost myself in the service of others? And if so, how can I accept it as a life well-lived, look in my own mirror, and rise?

⸸ May 13

...those with the brightest days do indeed suffer the darkest nights.

Chariots

There are some people you see that seem to streak through the sky like Apollo.

Chariots of fire, unstoppable. Illuminating all they come near. But what you don't see is what happens when the arc of the day is complete. When the horses are down, and everything is still.

The thing you never think about, no, never allow yourself to believe, is that those with the brightest days usually suffer the darkest nights. Yes, the height of success one achieves is often balanced by the depths of despair they endure.

So if you find yourself struggling, down, and walking through a darkness of your own, please keep going. Because there's a chariot and team of your own, just waiting for you around the bend, and your time to shine is surely coming.

Ask Yourself This...

How can I remind myself that the part of someone's life I see is just a fragment of their full story—that, like me, they too experience darkness, struggle, and unfulfilled dreams?

⸸ May 14

...offer all the love you can.

Planting Gardens
You move through life, leaving pieces of yourself in people and places.
In small conversations and deep dives—
each moment carrying a bit of your love.

So today, be mindful to leave only the best pieces out in the world and offer all the love you can.
Because what you say and do today, might someday make all the difference in the world to someone, somewhere.

Ask Yourself This...
Today, will I commit to being more intentional with my words and actions, spreading as much love as I can?

⸸ May 15

I hope people treat you well today.

Right now
It's just me and you—
me leaving words here,
you reading them when you can
It's just us.
So since we have this moment,
let's pause for a second,
drop our shoulders,
release that tightness in our guts,
And together, just take
One
Deep
Breath

There. Feel better?

I hope people treat you well today.
That you feel loved, acknowledged, and listened to.
And that whatever troubles are in your life, turn out to be short lived.

Thanks for spending these few seconds with me.
I appreciate it more than you'll ever know.

Ask Yourself This…
Who can I connect with in a meaningful way today to share even just a moment of peace, tranquility, and happiness?

⸸ May 16

...the world desperately needs you.

I Stand with You

To the empath navigating an unempathetic world—
Who feels life more deeply than most but has always been afraid to express it:
I stand with you.

I stand with your innocence,
Your strength,
Your heart,
Your resilience,
Your openness,
Your wonder,
And your old soul.
I stand with it all.

Because I know something you may not:
The world, though it may never admit it, desperately needs you.
It needs all your wonder,
All your caring,
All your tears,
And yes, every single bit of your innocence.

So don't hesitate or be afraid.
Care, love, and feel more deeply than you ever have.
Then take a deep breath—
And show the world what it truly means to be alive.

Ask Yourself This...

Isn't it time I accepted my inner wonder and innocence as the most beautiful part of who I am and honored it by sharing it with the world?

⸸ May 17

...you're worthy and more ready than you realize.

The Great Ones
It's time to finally accept that you are indeed one of the great ones.
That your gifts may be hidden, but are undeniable.
And you're worthy and more ready than you realize.
So please try to summon the courage to share what you know—
especially when you feel anything but courageous enough to do so.

But also acknowledge that you're this thing called "human",
and the emotional weight of being vulnerable enough to put your
passion and thoughts into the world is anything but light.

So be kind to yourself and give it time.
But don't you dare stop.
Because someone most definitely needs what you have to give,
in the way only you can give it.

Ask Yourself This...
Isn't it about time I accepted that I am indeed great in my own way, and that my thoughts, words, and perspectives are TRULY needed in the world?

⸸ May 18

Once you truly accept the fact that love is the only reason we're here, nothing is ever the same.

Ask Yourself This…
How can I change my thoughts, words, and actions to spread more love in my daily life?

May 19

...people who care and want to help if just given the chance.

Don't Go It Alone

If you're struggling, please remember—you don't have to do it alone. Because everyone could benefit from having someone to talk to more often than not.

So be honest. Be vulnerable. Let it out. You'll feel better, and in doing so, you'll help show that the world is filled with people who care and want to help—if only given the chance.

It's going to be ok.

Ask Yourself This…

Who in my life can I turn to when I'm struggling, and how can I connect more deeply with them so they know they can turn to me when they are as well?

♃ May 20

Make that one happen.

Tiny Dreams
What's the smallest dream you have?
Like, for the next hour, minute, or even just a second?
Think about what THAT dream looks like.
Make that one happen.
Then do it again, and again, and again…

Ask Yourself This…
Shouldn't I start to think about my goals and dreams not as distant and almost unattainable, but as things I can act upon
and make it happen now?

⸸ May 21

May the chaos of your mind be no match for the wisdom and brilliance of your soul.

Ask Yourself This…
What practices can I build into my day that will allow for the stillness needed for the brilliance of my soul to surface?

May 22

What could you lose yourself in doing for hours on end?

The Path
What is your highest alignment?
Where do you experience bliss and flow?
What is effortless, elevating, and energizing?
What could you lose yourself in doing for hours on end?

Trust that—
because the things that light you up might not be just simple joys, but the reason you're here.

Ask Yourself This…
What things do I enjoy doing so much that I lose track of time when doing them, and is there a way to make them more of a focus in my life?

May 23

Today you can decide to spread peace, love, and kindness, or not. So, what's it going to be?

Ask Yourself This…
No seriously, what's it going to be?

⸸ May 24

This is powerful.

The Most Important Question
The most important question isn't "How can I get what I want?"
but "How can I help others get what they need?"

Make this shift in perspective, and life will change in ways you could never have imagined.

Promise.

Ask Yourself This…
If I actually made this shift in perspective, how would it change my life and the lives of those around me?

⸸ May 25

...bring their blessings just a little closer to the surface.

Bring Them There
Whatever you can do—
To help someone feel more deeply, appreciate life just a little more, and bring their blessings just a little closer to the surface…

Do that.

Because the deeper we feel, connect, and love,
The closer we bring each other to experiencing life with less judgment, expectation, ego, and control—the better off we'll be.

So please, start looking for those opportunities, and take them.

Ask Yourself This…
What is just one simple thing I can do today to make someone feel loved, acknowledged, and seen, and more importantly, will I do it?

⸸ May 26

Think about those stories and what they say about you.

Stories
What stories are you using to define yourself to the world?
And more importantly, why?

We all have our go-to stories.
The ones from our past we bring out to entertain, amaze, and inspire.
Think about those stories and what they say about you.

More importantly, ask yourself why, out of all the stories you could share, you feel these are the ones that represent you the best and make the list?

Think about what it says about you,
then ask if these stories are still the truest reflection not only of who you are, but what you want to be.

Ask Yourself This…
Do the stories I tell align with the person I want to be and the life I want to live, or is it time to redefine my narrative?

May 27

Just like a heartbeat.

Simplicity and Elegance
If we can learn anything from nature, it's that we were meant to live simple, elegant lives.

Look no further than a leaf, a blade of grass, or a bird in flight, and you will see an impossibly complex yet effortlessly functional design.
Just like breathing.
Just like a heartbeat.
Just being.

Take a moment to examine the things that bring you stress and worry. Identify the aspects of your life that are neither simple nor elegant, and scrutinize them to determine if they are truly worthy of your time, energy, and attention.

So breathe.
Simplify.
Surround yourself with people and things grounded in simplicity
and rise to the level of elegance that you were meant to have.
Then watch your life soar.

Ask Yourself This...
Who and what bring simplicity and elegance to my life, and how can I invite more of that in?

⸸ May 28

Do something nice for Near-Future You. Near-Future You deserve it.

Ask Yourself This...
What am I going to do for "Near-Future Me" Today?

May 29

Action breaks the grip of what keeps us down.

Move

You're going to get up.
You're going to rise.
Not because you want to,
Not because you need to,
But because you have to.
It's inevitable.
It's just the way life works.

But the time it takes for that to happen is in your control.
It's about perspective.
It's about mindset.
It's about the decision to take action and move.

That last part—action and movement—is the key.
Action breaks the grip of what holds us down, and *any* movement immediately crushes stagnation and relieves hopelessness.

Why?
Because movement is hope, aspiration, and the first step on your path to revival.
So don't just sit there waiting for something to happen.
Don't let what brought you down be the thing that keeps you there.
Do one small thing.
Just one.
Please, just take that tiny step.
And move.

Ask Yourself This…

What small thing can I do today to break the grip of stagnation and get me on the path I really want to take?

⸸ May 30

Because it's only on the floor that you'll find a surface hard enough to push from.

Rock Bottom
Today I'm not going to tell you to breathe or relax, or that everything will be ok...
I'm not going to remind you that you're doing a great job or that it's the simple things that matter...
I'm not going to talk about love
Acts of kindness, or the power of gratitude.
No, I'm not going to say any of that today.

Because I know that sometimes you need understanding and empathy more than a cheerleader or perspective.
You need someone to agree with you that life might suck right now and that sometimes nothing seems to matter.
I get it.
It's important to feel it all.
To go there and sometimes even sink far enough to touch rock bottom.
Because it's only there you'll find a surface hard enough to push from.

Yes, life does suck sometimes.
And if it sucks for you now,
I'm sorry.
I'm sorry for your pain, your stress, and your sadness. I'm sorry for your uncertainty, worry, and doubt.
But know that in the long run, it will all eventually subside, and you'll be just fine.
Different for sure, but still, just fine.
Promise.

Ask Yourself This...
How can I honor where I am right now without making myself wrong or rushing to feel better?

⳨ May 31

Just do your best.
That's all you can do.

⸸ June 1

Be the one sitting back, looking inward.

Placing Blame
We spend so much of our time placing blame—
holding others accountable for what they did or didn't do,
or for who they are or who they aren't.

But often the things we criticize in others are reflections of what we see as deficiencies in ourselves.

It's a deflection, it's safe, and most of all,
a reason not to do the work we know deep down we need to do.

So instead of placing blame, look in the mirror and take accountability for what you see.

Nobody can do this work but you.
Nobody is responsible but you.
And certainly nobody has the power but you.

So while the rest of the world is finding fault,
Be the one sitting back, looking inward, and sitting in the honesty of what really matters.

Ask Yourself This…
How did the thought that the things I find fault with in others are most likely the very things I do not like about myself make me feel?
Do I accept or reject it, and why?

June 2

Just know that whatever condition you find yourself in,
I've thought of you.

Today
Maybe you've awoken with so much love for life you could cry,
or sadly those tears are coming from a darker place...
Maybe you're ready to conquer the world,
or honestly, just "can't even" right now…

So whether we're the closest of friends
or just connected here in this moment with our paths never to cross again,
just know that I've thought of you, appreciated you're here,
and yes, already sent you some love.

Ask Yourself This…
How can I remind myself that I am deserving of love and compassion, even on the days when I feel disconnected or down?

June 3

Does my existence move the needle of humanity even the slightest bit in the right direction?

Your Little Corner
You go about your life—washing dishes,
raising children, going to work.
All the while, you see others on grand stages,
elevated to unimaginable heights,
and you wonder,
"Am I significant?"
"If I weren't here to wash this dish,
or do the work that a million others could do,
would it even matter?"
"Does my existence move the needle of humanity, even in the slightest?"

The truth is, every single one of us is a tiny gear
in an impossibly complex machine.
Each with a purpose in the grand scheme.
Each integral to its success.
We're all here at the right time,
in the right capacity,
to make life move as it should—
and to allow Love to flow where it needs to.

So tend to your little corner of life.
Tend it well.
Because you have no idea
how grand of a stage you're really on.

Ask Yourself This…
How can I find more meaning and purpose in the everyday tasks and responsibilities that make up my "little corner" of life?

June 4

Take the opportunity to ask questions and understand.

Resistance and Fear
Opposition to a new idea is often not true resistance but rather a lack of understanding and yes, sometimes an expression of fear.

So instead of rushing to prove yourself right,
take the opportunity to ask questions and gain clarity on the issue and the driving force behind it.

Do this and you'll not only learn why your idea was being rejected, but also build trust through acknowledgement, respect, and curiosity.

And that's always a good thing.

Ask Yourself This...
How often do I get defensive, and could it be that it truly is a reflection of the fear I have of rejection, vulnerability, or loss of control?

June 5

...the time in this dark place is coming to an end.

The Slow Rise
Do you feel it?
That one dim flicker of light?
That first feeling that things are starting to rise?
Almost imperceptible,
but still, a sense from some deep, knowing place -
That the time in this dark space is nearing its end,
That tomorrow might be brighter than today,
and yes, that things are going to be okay.

Maybe you don't, and no matter how hard you try to feel it,
the flicker isn't there.

But just wait.

Because one of life's universal truths is that whatever falls,
inevitably must rise.
And surely, you will.

Ask Yourself This...
When I think back to the hardest times in my past, how long did it take for it to rise up from darkness, and what lessons did I learn along the way?

⸸ June 6

Failure is inevitable.
What you do next
is what really matters.

Ask Yourself This…

When I fail to achieve something I've set out to do, how can I train myself to pivot to the next step vs falling into negativity?

⸸ June 7

I think we should just meet for coffee instead.

Dis-Connected
Can you hear me now?
What about now?
Is anyone there?
I think I'm in a bad cell.

I think we're all in a bad cell.

Talking into nothing,
Words going nowhere,
Hearing the distant crackle of what we hope is a friend—
Disconnected.
Can you hear me now?

Maybe we should just meet for coffee instead.

Ask Yourself This…
How can I prioritize real-life interactions in today's age, and what is one step I can take to have meaningful, face-to-face moments with others?

June 8

You don't deserve more than what you're willing to give.

Deserving
What do you feel you deserve simply for existing?
What do you believe you should get from those you love,
from the world at large and from life itself, just for being you?

Before you answer, I must ask, do you think you deserve anything more than what you're *willing* to give?

Should you expect—or even feel entitled—to have others rise above your own threshold of giving just because you are you?

I would say no, none of us do.

Notice I said "willing" and not "able."
Most of us go through times—or may even live in circumstances—where we are not able to give.
Where our situations prevent us from sharing our talents, and our time.
But that doesn't mean we aren't willing.
In fact, those who aren't able sometimes are the most willing, because they've experienced lack and want desperately to share abundance.

So if life feels abundant and you're not struggling beyond the norm,
focus on what you're willing to give.
Let go of your own needs and turn toward others. Because in doing so, you'll *truly* deserve all the goodness coming your way.

Ask Yourself This…
Do I agree with this take on "deserving," and if not, what feelings did this bring up in me that I should explore?

June 9

...you've solved every problem you've ever had in life—by yourself.

Nobody is Coming

Nobody is coming to solve your problems. It's true.
Yes, you can share what you're going through and receive infinite thoughts, prayers, and encouragement.
You can seek support, friendship, and advice from your community.
But at the end of the day, if you are to get past what you're facing, it's just you who has to stand up, find the strength, and do what it takes to move your life from here to there.

Because nobody is coming but you.

I know that might sound lonely, overwhelming, and maybe even impossible at times—and maybe it is.
But let's be honest: you've literally solved every problem you've ever faced in your life—by yourself.

Now you might point to the times when someone stepped in and altered your course, or even intervened to help you through troubled times.
But even then, it was just you.
You who attracted them into your life.
You who showed up in ways that inspired them to help.
You who took what they had to offer and put it into action.
Just you.

So no, nobody is coming.
But they never have before.
It's always been just you who made it through.
Every. Single. Time.

Ask Yourself This…

How does this thought that I alone have been ultimately responsible for every positive change in my life make me feel? Do I accept it or reject it, and why?

⸸ June 10

Let them dissipate on the slightest breeze.

Troubles and Tragedies
Troubles come and go.
They're the kinds of things that affect us in the moment, and are processed so quickly, we can't recall them two weeks later.
In the moment, they command all of our attention, thought, and energy, but dissipate as quickly as clouds in the wind.

Tragedies stay with us forever.
They are the things that carry dates and times.
We know where we were and what we were doing.
We can smell, taste, see, and hear all of it down to the smallest detail.
These are the big things,
the life-changing things,
the things we wish never were, and would do anything to erase.

But lately, I see people treating troubles as if they were tragedies.
Doing all they can to keep the wind at bay until the sky becomes so filled with these burdens that the sun struggles to break through.

And this is a tragedy in and of itself.
A tragedy of wasted life, loss of perspective, missed opportunity, and fun.

So let your troubles dissipate on the slightest breeze, so when a tragedy does come your way, you'll have more sunny days than not,
to look back upon and smile.

Ask Yourself This...
How often do I treat my troubles as tragedies, and how does this affect my daily state of being?

June 11

...it's time to take out the hammer and break free.

What Are You Afraid Of?
That moment—you know the one...
That split second when you want to show your authentic self.
That fleeting feeling of safety, courage, or "I don't care what anyone thinks!" bravado, quickly followed by an inner admonishment or a spike of fear so fierce that it will be a long while before your authentic self dares to try *that* again.

So what are you afraid of?

I'm guessing you probably only have answers that live on the surface:
"I'm too this or that."
"I have nothing to say."
"I'm uninteresting."
"I'm awkward."
"I'm shy."
"I'm just not like everyone else."
"And who wants to hear what I have to say anyway?"

Well, I do. because, like everyone else, you were born with something we need to hear and a purpose you're on your way to discovering.

Maybe it's time to believe that the world *does* want and need you. Not the version you've been pretending to be or the one you've convinced yourself they want, but the *real* you.
I think it's about time.
And the time is now.

Ask Yourself This...
Why am I trying to be what I think the world wants me to be, and what can I do today to start being my true self without any regrets?

⸸ June 12

I need to be taken to that place.

Drift
Heal me.
Take me in your arms and make me whole.
Take me from this.
Hold me.
Protect me.
Tell me it's going to be okay.
Make me believe it's true.
Let me rest my head on you, my eyes closed,
listening to your heartbeat,
surrounded by the safety of everything you are.

I need to be taken to that place.
Where I don't have to worry,
where I don't have a care,
and all I have to do is drift,
breathe, and know you're there to set me free.

We all need that person or place that brings a sense of overwhelming calm, peace, and security to our lives.
And I hope you have or find yours.

Ask Yourself This…
Who in my life brings me a sense of calm, peace, and security, and how can I spend more time with them?

June 13

Maybe it's time you gave "fine" a rest.

Fine

Fine usually isn't fine, now is it?
It's really just a way to say you're walking that tightrope between "barely good" and "really not ok."
It's both a plea and a pass.
A plea to be asked how you really are
And a pass to anyone who'd rather not engage.

Maybe it's time you gave "fine" a rest
and use all the other words that describe how you *really are* instead.

You might be surprised how much better your life will become if you do.

Ask Yourself This...

What would happen if I were actually more honest about how I'm doing?

⸸ June 14

You just weren't wired to sit and think.

Trading Time
Was it worth it?
All these things you traded your time for—
running to all of your somewheres in pursuit of somethings or someones. Never keeping still to appreciate the life you'd already built.

But no, that was impossible.
You just weren't wired to sit still.
To be in just one place, with one person, doing one thing
No, that just wasn't you
But don't you think maybe it's time to slow down, and accept what you already have is enough?

Ask Yourself This…
Am I ready to stop myself treating everything as equally important, and prioritize the use of my time on the things that matter most?

⸸ June 15

What are you holding back from the world?

Dams

We've become expert dam builders.
Constructing complex, fortified structures of fear and insecurity that hold back everything we are meant to share with the world.
So strong are these that our hopes, dreams, and very purpose in life can all rise without so much as a drop *ever* making it to the other side.

What we often fail to realize is that for all our effort, energy, and time spent holding back what was meant to flow freely, we're creating a drought of epic proportions—a drought of thought, love, inspiration, connectedness, achievement, and learning.

We see the results every day: billions of dams holding back trillions of dreams across the globe, keeping what should be flourishing on floodplains locked away upstream.

So, what's behind your dam?
What are you holding back from the world?
Perhaps it's time to stop adding height and let at least some of it, pour over the top.

Ask Yourself This...

What is my dam made of, why is it there, and most importantly, what can I do today to start taking it down?

⸸ June 16

Yes, it's time for me to finally listen to myself with the rapt attention I've given only to others.

Listening

You know you're in there somewhere.
The real you.
The peaceful you.
The you that was born into this world with a gift to give and a difference to make.
Not like what you've become.
Tired, frustrated, and worn down,
lost in to-do lists and responsibilities,
living in service to everyone but yourself.
And you find yourself asking, "Who am I, why am I here, and more importantly, what's next?"

And this scares you because you were sure you'd know by now,
and the fear it's brought up in you can feel paralyzing at times.

So, it's finally time to break the cycle you've been in for so long
and let surface what has been hidden inside for all these years.

And it all starts by listening—not to the advice of others, but yourself,
and doing so with the rapt attention you've given only to others.

So yes, the time has come for you to simply be still, hear what your
heart has to say, and step into who you really are.

Ask Yourself This…

What is one thing I can do today to create the stillness needed to begin truly listening to myself, and where can I find some direction on how to begin?

♰ June 17

Life will always take you to unexpected places, at unexpected times, and at its own pace.

Amusement Park: A True Story (As Best As I Can Recall…)
I'm 6 years old—
waiting in line for my turn to ride the Fireball Racers.
Real Engine.
Real Gas Pedal.
And I can really steer too!

But I didn't see the track underneath,
and I didn't know it only went so fast.

So regardless of how many times I turned that wheel,
my racer only went 12" to the left and 12" to the right and stayed exactly the same distance from that white number 5 car I was so sure I'd pass when the attendant dropped that flag.`

It was frustrating!

I wanted to race past the Cotton Candy Mountain,
but ended up in Gumdrop Falls.
I thought I'd sneak past that Number 5 in Grimstone Canyon,
but stayed politely behind as we cruised by Mr. Phipps General Store.

But when we finally finished, and even though I never got what I thought I wanted, I ran right back in line for another turn.
Why?
Because I realized that Cotton Candy Mountain was actually pretty cool, and the guy gave me a free mini Hershey's just for *passing* Mr. Phipps General Store.

Who knew that this one ride at the amusement park would turn out to be a life lesson I'd only realize years later while watching my own kids "drive" those cars.

So keep that pedal down and do your best to stay centered.
And accept that regardless of your best-laid plans, intentions, or the energy you spend trying to steer your course,
life will always take you to unexpected places,
at unexpected times,
and at its own pace.

Truly accept this, and you'll discover that life not only has fun surprises in store for you, but will also turn out to be one hell of a ride.

Ask Yourself This…
How control-driven am I, and isn't it about time I started dropping my expectations and accepting the unfolding of life as it comes?

⸸ June 18

Do I really have the energy it will take to get to those branches?

How High Should I Climb?
There's this level.
Then the level above…
and above…
and above…
The question is, do you settle in and rest, or continue to climb?

Maybe you're wondering that right now.

The low-hanging fruit has been picked.
And now all you can see seems far out of reach.
So ask yourself, do I really have the energy to get to those branches?
Or should I just be happy I'm here, savor the fruit, and enjoy the view?

Ask Yourself This…
Looking around at all the other things I could be doing with my life, is it worth it to continue to climb, or is here ok for now?

⸸ June 19

It was better than OK, not quite as nice as good...

On the Way to Fine

I met you on the way to Fine.
You were tired and bruised.
I was worn and bleeding.
But once our paths converged, we were inseparable.
We walked side by side, helping each other up one hill then another, ate together under shady trees, and sweated it out under the hot sun.

We'd both heard a lot about Fine.
It was better than OK,
but not *quite* as nice as Good.
We were told it was wide, flat, and vast.
Nothing too high or low in Fine.
Nothing too exciting or perilous in Fine.
Nobody ever got rich in Fine.
But nobody ever failed miserably either.

Fine might be a bit boring.
But after my living in Hard Times for a while, and your growing up in Turmoil, Fine seemed like paradise, and we couldn't wait to get there and settle in for a good long time.

But as we crested that final ridge, and Fine rose slowly out of the horizon, we somehow shared the same thought and stopped dead in our tracks.
Never speaking a word, and with only a knowing glance, we agreed that remaining in Fine just wouldn't do, and just passed through as quickly as we could, on a direct path, to Great.

Ask Yourself This...

How long have I been living in Fine, and isn't it about time I moved to Great?

June 20

It's times like these that you downshift into that lower gear.

Downshift

There are times when 5th gear is fine.
You're on level grade and the road is paved, smooth, and wide.
There's an ease to the day-to-day, and opportunities are easy to see.
These are the times when you make progress, expand your life, and move quickly in the direction of your dreams.

But then there are times that call not for speed, but power.
When the hills are steep, and if there is a road at all, it's narrow, treacherous, and terrifyingly unpredictable, and you find yourself slowed by fear because you know it's up to you and you only—and the guardrails were taken down long ago.
It's times like these that you downshift into that lower gear.
The one you use when times get tough and the passing scenery doesn't matter, because your eyes are fixed directly in front of you.
Progress is not mile by mile but inch by inch, and if you stop, getting stuck will be the least of your problems. Because backsliding will be disastrous.

So inch by inch it is.
All of your power to the wheels you pray will gain traction.
All of your skill to maintain forward motion
Laser-focused intent to keep going and get through to a time
when 5th gear will once again make sense.

So know what gear you're supposed to be in, understand when it's time to shift, and most importantly, stay on the road!

Ask Yourself This…

Do I find it hard to slow down, reevaluate, and shift gears when I need to, or does my expectation that "Life is a highway" get in the way? (Apologies, I just couldn't resist the 80's song reference…)

June 21

You might just have stumbled upon your true purpose.

The Worker and the Wiser
We have two voices—our Minds (the Worker) and Souls (the Wiser).

The Worker pushes ahead—harder, faster, often to the point of exhaustion. Trying to control the situation, keep us safe, and always push us in the direction it *thinks* we should go.

The Wiser taps into a deeper, universal truth— fueled by love, faith, hope, and the understanding that *life unfolds as it should.* And that the creases in our plans are not just temporary, but essential for growth.

Most of the time, these two forces clash.
The Worker races forward, fixated on immediate tasks and outcomes, the Wiser holding back, urging patience and perspective.
It's a constant struggle—one driven by urgency, the other by faith.

But in rare moments, they find harmony.
No tug-of-war.
No inner friction.
They rise together, working as one to guide us toward our purpose or through challenges we might not otherwise overcome.
The Worker creates plans; the Wiser makes them possible.
The Worker brings energy; the Wiser channels it to where it's needed.

These are times of flow and expansion. They come when your actions align with what you were meant to do. So if you feel this synergy—if you wake up balanced, energized, and motivated—pay close attention. You might just be on the verge of something big.

Ask Yourself This...
Can you remember those times when The Worker and The Wiser were working in harmony with each other, and if so, what were you doing?

⸸ June 22

Prepare yourself for the day when you're not motivated.

Trusting the Process

You're excited but nervous.
You love who you're becoming, but you've been here before—
You had fits and starts, holding on for as long as you could, but each time, there was a fall. Sometimes it was slow, but more often than not, it was a dramatic, unexpected turn in the wrong direction.

Now, here you are—smiling, rising higher with each day.
You're doing things you've never done, finding blue skies above the clouds, but always keeping one eye on the ever-shrinking ground below, because you can't stop reminding yourself you're *terrified* of heights.

So today I'm here to remind you that there *will* be turbulence, and ultimately, a small or even significant turn downwards.
So expect it, and more importantly, prepare for it.
Prepare yourself for the day when you're not motivated, the times when old fears try to bring you down, and those moments of self-doubt.

Go there now. Understand what that looks like. Journal.
Write your future doubting, unmotivated, "I knew it wouldn't last" self a note letting them know you understand how they feel, but under no circumstances are they to go back to the place you just came from.
Give them inspiration, hope, and love… and then some direction.

Help them get through it because the you who is soaring now deserves a higher floor. You've worked hard, and you're doing it. So don't you dare stop (and that goes for future you as well).

Ask Yourself This…

When will I commit to writing to my future self to ensure I stay on track?

⸸ June 23

Granite and Marble have nothing on you.

Cornerstone
Granite or Marble I am not.
Yet I've put myself in this place—
becoming the foundation on which the rest of this house will be built.

Why would I do this to myself—and the people who will live here—
when I'm so porous? Soaking in every bit of rain that comes my way,
and getting weaker with every storm…

Do you know how that feels?
When your strength seems insignificant to the weight you must bear?

Somehow though, you always make it through.
Porous as you may think you are,
the truth is that Granite and Marble,
have nothing on you.

Ask Yourself This…
If I'm as weak and unprepared as I'm telling myself I am, then how have I gotten through literally every challenge that's come my way?

June 24

It's not vast and overpowering but strong, lasting, and personal.

This Little Light of Yours...
Maybe you see it as a spotlight—
trying to illuminate everything it touches,
and stretching as far as the eye can see.

But perhaps it's time to see your light differently.
Not vast and overpowering,
but strong, lasting, and personal.
Not a torch, but an eternal flame.

Yes, your light is meant to spread far and wide,
to go wherever darkness is, and do all the things
love would do if just given the chance.

But to do that, the spreading must be through others,
not just you.

So maybe it's time to realize that its true power is in
illuminating single rooms, where people can gather, sit,
and feel safe enough to share life on a deeper level.

Yes, if you focus it correctly,your little light
can shine both *bright* and *forever* in the
hearts, souls, and minds of those you love,
and well beyond.

Ask Yourself This...
How can I focus my light where it matters most and trust others to carry it forward?

⸸ June 25

...breathe into the life that's waiting for you just around the bend.

It Doesn't Matter

It doesn't matter who you are, how many times you've fallen, or how few times you've found the strength to rise.

It doesn't matter that you've made mistakes, lost your way, or done things you now regret.

And it definitely doesn't matter the condition you find yourself in as you're reading this.

What does matters is that after all of it,
you've made the decision to be right here with me
in this moment.

So hopefully, this can be the start of something good—
that the words I've left for you in this book will resonate, and you can finally begin to forgive yourself, accept yourself, let go of the past, and step into the life you so richly deserve.

Ask Yourself This...

What can I do today to start a journey of self-grace, acceptance, and love?

⸸ June 26

I promise to do the hard work.

Tentative Steps
I'm taking the first steps out of the darkness—
ones that are small, important, and long overdue.
To be honest, they are being taken on faith and trust alone.
But faith is fine for now, and trust is a much-needed companion.

So I promise to do the hard work.
To care enough about myself to do my best every day.
To look more to the future than the past.
And replace faith and trust,
with the habits and skills of the person I'm becoming.

I've got this.

Ask Yourself This…
What small steps can I take today to move forward from a challenging situation?

June 27

The answers that you've been searching in so many places for are there, just waiting to be heard.

You Already Know
There's no magic in these words.
Nothing here will suddenly move you from "here" to "there", or put you on a different path. Because deep down, you already know where you're going and what it takes to get there.

I'm talking, of course, about what's coming from your soul—the deepest part of you that has always been there, whispering the truth, waiting for you to release the need for control and surrender to what's already within you.

So quiet your mind and go within.
Let go of the urge to force things
and simply listen.

The answers you've been searching for—the ones you've looked for in so many places—are already there, just waiting for you to hear them.

Ask Yourself This…
How can you create more space in my life to get quiet and truly listen to the wisdom within me?

⸸ June 28

Believe that the truth of who you are is enough, just as it is.

Truth

The act of separating your true self from the one you've meticulously crafted to protect yourself over the course of your life is one of the hardest things you'll ever do.

It can be terrifying—if you let it.

But if you approach this work with deep self-love, commit to releasing the past and embracing the future, and treat yourself with the same kindness, gentleness, and patience you would offer the infant you once were, then you'll finally begin to discover who you were before the world told you who you should be.

So be still.

Love yourself so deeply that the protective layers are no longer needed. Accept yourself so completely that the opinions of others will never again hold power over you.

Believe that the truth of who you are is enough, just as it is.
And promise yourself that, from now on, the world will finally see, love, and appreciate the real you.

Please do this—because the world truly needs to meet the real you.
Once again.

Ask Yourself This...

What tiny step will I take today (and I do mean tiny) to start revealing my true self to the world?

⸸ June 29

If only you could see yourself through my eyes for just a moment.

Lenses
I think we're seeing two different things...
Maybe your mirror is defective?
Or perhaps the optometrist got your prescription wrong?
Because from what I've been told, my eyesight is just fine,
and what I see when I look at you is simply *beautiful.*

So maybe you should take another look,
because for the life of me, I can't understand how you see it any other way.

Ask Yourself This…
Isn't it about time I looked not for the imperfections but for the beauty in myself?

⸸ June 30

Where did this light come from?

Smile
I saw you smile today—
A different smile than before.
A smile with confidence behind it,
One that matched the light in your eyes.
Yes, this smile was different,
Because there was no trace of sadness,
No asterisk like the ones from recent days.

So, what changed?
Where did this light come from?
And more importantly, how do you plan to keep it on?

Ask Yourself This…
What makes me truly smile, and how do I bring more of that into my life?

⸸ July 1

Maybe it's time to just trust that the chef knows what he's doing.

Just So

It seems you want life to be "just so"—
A little of this,
not too much of that,
and definitely NONE of that other thing.
It's as if you're viewing your life like a menu at a restaurant, and you're the pickiest eater there:
"I'll have the Chicken Parm, but with half the breading, mozzarella instead of parm, light sauce, and just a few mushrooms on the side—not the seasoned ones, though. And can you make sure the chicken is REALLY thin?"

But life's chef doesn't work like that.
He cooks up masterpieces that are nuanced in flavor,
unexpected in complexity,
and impossible to understand.
And there you are, with your expectations and false sense of control.
Asking to change the recipe to your liking,
then somehow expecting it to show up "just so."

Maybe it's time to trust that the chef knows what he's doing,
and simply, enjoy the meal.

Ask Yourself This…

How often do I try to control situations instead of just going with the flow with a positive attitude?

July 2

I think I might even be writing this to distract myself.

Distracted
I'm using work to distract myself.
I'm using food to distract myself.
I'm using TV to distract myself.
I'm using the news to distract myself.
I'm using the thought of working out to distract myself.
I'm using the regret that I didn't work out to distract myself.
I'm using the practice of replaying what I said to others to distract myself.
I'm using the feeling of regret for things said and unsaid to distract myself.
I'm using the construct of a lack of time to distract myself.
I'm using judgment to distract myself.
I'm using being there for others to distract myself.
I'm using the past to distract myself.
I'm using the future to distract myself.
I'm using worry to distract myself.
I'm using how I feel about others to distract myself.
I'm using how I feel about myself to distract myself.
I'm using my self-righteous opinions to distract myself.
I'm using "being busy" to distract myself.
I think I might even be writing this to distract myself…
So maybe it's time to stop distracting myself and finally get down to the work of quieting my mind, going inward, and discovering what I'm distracting myself from, and more importantly, why.

What about you?

Ask Yourself This…
What am I distracting myself with, and more importantly,
What am I avoiding?

⸸ July 3

I guess it's time to finally start cleaning out the fridge.

Leftovers

The things that are holding you back—the bad habits, old triggers, and limiting beliefs from your past—
They have nothing to do with where you are now, who you've become, or where you're headed.

They're just remnants from a different time, mindset, and set of circumstances you've held on to.
Old leftovers, forgotten in the back of life's refrigerator.
Nothing more, nothing less.

So maybe it's time to finally clean out the fridge,
let go of what no longer serves you, and make space for something, fresh off the grill.

Ask This...

What old "leftovers" from my past am I holding on to, and what will I do today to make room for new growth and possibilities?

⸸ July 4

You've come too far just to crash now.

Gravity
Filled with fuel. Pent-up energy. All systems check.
Countdown begins: 5, 4, 3, 2—1!
Chains break, and the ground quakes.
I'm off! No turning back now!

…Pulse quickens
"This is happening."

…Almost breathless
"I'm doing it!"

…The horizon expands
"I never knew it was possible."

…Booster rockets fall away
"Am I on my own?"

…Slowing, just a bit
"Was this a mistake?"

…Fuel gauge drops
"This can't be right..."

…A tilt
"What was that?"

…Earth, now just a marble
"What have I done?!"

…Another tilt
"I'm going to die! ABORT!"

Voices call out—my team, my support—
"Hit the switch!"
"You're running out of time!"
"You have to act NOW!"

My hand is frozen…
Another tilt…
The horizon again...
Gravity taking hold.

I guess you're the only one who can finish this story.
I really hope you hit that switch, engage the power,
and make it into orbit—
Because you've come way too far just to crash now.

Ask Yourself This...
What critical "switch" am I hesitating to hit, and what is stopping me from taking the action I need to move forward?

⸸ July 5

You've been through and overcome so much.

Some Thoughts on Failure...
You *are* your past "failures."
Every single one of them, and all they were made of.
And that's a great thing.
Because they weren't *failures—*
they were *lessons*,
Each filled with the wisdom you've gained to be better today.

So to see them as anything less than the foundation you're building your life on would waste all the time, pain, and emotional energy you poured into what didn't go as planned.

It's time to start building yourself up again.
Look at the person in the mirror as someone who keeps trying, learning, and moving forward—because that's who you are.

You've been through and overcome so much.
Now it's time to mine that gold.

You've got this.

Ask Yourself This…
Pick some "failures" you've beaten yourself up over or regretted throughout the years. What are the lessons you learned from these experiences?

⸸ July 6

The truth is that if your intent is pure, then so are your words and actions.

The Best of Intent
One of life's everyday tragedies is our tendency to spin the unexpected reactions of others into stories about what we should have said or done differently.

This can leave us feeling wrong, resentful, lesser, and even unworthy. The truth is that if your intent is pure, then so are your words and actions. And that's all that truly matters.

Ask Yourself This…
What would happen if I accepted that I'm doing my best, recognized that I won't always say or do the perfect thing—and was okay with that?

⸸ July 7

It will just take some extra time.

How I Became Patient

I used to struggle with patience.
And by "struggle," I mean I had almost none at all.

If something wasn't coming together, or unexpectedly taking too long, I could just feel the frustration and anxiety surging inside me.
And that was something I really didn't like about myself.

What's worse, I had no clue how to change it.
Until one day...

I don't know what I was working on, but one thing after another went wrong, and I could feel it happening again.
Then it occurred to me—all of this pressure was self-inflicted, and it all came down to my *need for control.*

The fact was that I was doing my very best, and things were simply taking a bit longer—that's all.

So now, when I start to feel that way, I remind myself that at some point in the future the problem will be solved or the task will be completed, and to get to that point, I just need to keep trying.
So in my mind, it's *already done*— I just need to get there.

That mindset shift was so powerful for me, and I know it will help you as well.

Ask Yourself This…

How can I remind myself of the thought of "*some point* " when I start becoming impatient?

⸸ July 8

Her Royal Highness to find a new title.

The Worrier Princess
She sits in her tower,
fretting about this and that—
things not in order,
things not done,
things that might happen and things that might not.

There's darkness around the corner, and the other shoe is always about to drop (glass slippers break easily, you know, and those shards will surely cut deep).

Though she's been waiting for a knight in shining armor to save her from the constant attacks of the ruthless armies in her mind, she really doesn't need saving at all. She just needs to look in the mirror and realize that her predictions of the future rarely come to pass.

Maybe it's time for Her Royal Highness to find a new title—one that reflects not who she is and what she fears, but who she's becoming, and the dragons she'll surely slay along the way.

Ask Yourself This…
How many things have I worried about that have actually come true?

July 9

The simple, beautiful, truth of you.

The Truth
Today, I'd like you to think about the truth.
Not about telling others the truth or even "showing up authentically," but about deep, personal truth.

The truth you've known since the day you were born.
The soft, powerful truth that has remained unchanged throughout every triumph and tragedy.

You know what I'm talking about — the simple, beautiful truth of *you*.

The truth you've kept hidden.
The truth you haven't believed.
The truth you've let life push aside time and again.

I'm thinking now is time you to take a deep breath, reconnect with it, and finally accept that who you are and what you bring to the world is inherently more beautiful, than what you've been willing to show.

Ask Yourself This…
Isn't it about time I reconnected with my deep, inner self?

⸸ July 10

...what if I told you there's a secret path to freedom?

Escape
Do you ever feel like your mind is working to sabotage your progress?
Guarding you so closely that you barely have space to move?
In those times, it seems to exist solely to keep you from growing—
crushing your goals like grapes,
and destroying your dreams with just a glance.

Strangely enough, this relentless guard believes it's protecting you
from the failure and hardship that will surely follow
if you step out of the comfort zone you've known for so long.

But what if I told you there's a secret path to freedom,
and a way to slip away unnoticed?

It all starts with tiny actions—
a single, deliberate step,
then another, and another.
Your mind thinks this is just fine,
and will never even know you've changed a thing,
until your life becomes beautifully unrecognizable.

Ask Yourself This...
What small step can I take today to begin my journey to freedom?

⸸ July 11

Believe that there is a grand plan for your life.

Life Always Finds a Way

Maybe this finds you wondering how it will all work out.
Racking your brain, running scenarios
Treating your problems like a math equation that can be "proved"
And each time, you step back from the blackboard frustrated.
Take out your eraser, and try again.

But there's one crucial thing you're leaving out.

Faith.
The trust that life is working for you even when it seems it's out to prove it's not. The belief there's a grand plan, one that will unfold if you wait long enough and allow it to happen.

The part of life so complex, no human has ever been able to explain it.

Yes, the larger your challenges, the more faith, patience, resilience, surrender, softness, the suspension of ego, and the relinquishment of control need all to be included, sometimes in amounts that may seem unreasonable.

So keep filling the blackboard
Work your plan, and prove your theories
But never forget to have some faith
That at the end of the day
Life always finds a way.

Ask Yourself This...

What proof do I have from my past that life always finds a way? (And if you're thinking "None," try again…)

⸸ July 12

Happiness isn't a destination, it's a practice.

Ask Yourself This…
What is one enjoyable habit I can start to bring happiness into my day?

July 13

...accept the fact, once and for all, that I'm only human.

Work in Progress
I'm trying my best, and that's all I can do.
Trying to do and say the right things,
show up for others in the right way at the right time,
and become the version of myself I know I can be.

But I fail every day.
Fail at being present enough to enjoy the small things in life.
Fail at clearly communicating my thoughts and intent.
Fail at slowing down enough to feel I'm doing more than just "trying."

Trying and failing, over and over and over again.
Day in, day out.
It's exhausting.
But it doesn't have to be, and it's time to make that shift in perspective.

It's time to give myself the self-love I need, the grace I deserve, and the forgiveness I extend so freely to everyone else. It's time to finally accept that my perception is probably off, that "failure" is subjective, and that I'm doing much more than trying—I'm persevering.
Finding new ways, opening up with every step and stumble, and most importantly, succeeding more than I'm willing to admit.

So I will continue to try, but I'll see those "failures" through a lens of self-love, acceptance, learning, grace, and forgiveness. I will take that long overdue breath, release the unrealistic standards and expectations I have for myself, and finally, open my eyes to how successful I truly am.

Ask Yourself This...
In what ways can I show myself the same compassion, forgiveness, and understanding I give others?

⸸ July 14

Sometimes it takes reengaging with the past to reimagine the future.

Untangled

Somewhere in the past, something happened to the through line of your life—a careless misstep that caused a kink when you were young, a career that stretched it to the point of breaking, and people who demanded slack in your line so theirs could remain tight.

Unfortunately, it got so tangled that when you were actually ready to try, you saw nothing but a dense ball of loops and twists, leaving you unsure where to start the unraveling.

And you felt angry and resentful, wondering why others seemed to have straight and true lines, when yours was such a mess.
So you stopped trying.

Rather than put in the meticulous work of pulling it apart bit by bit, you told yourself it was just "life" and went about your days doing things you weren't meant to do, with people you weren't supposed to be with, and in pursuit of things you weren't meant to have. So the tangles grew worse and the ball got bigger, until one day it became impossible to ignore any longer.
And here you are.

So now what do you do?
You think back to the last moment your life felt on track, cut the line, and pull *that* thread forward. Because sometimes it takes reengaging with the past, to reimagine the future.

So get out your scissors, cut the line, and begin again.

Ask Yourself This...

When was the last time I felt my life was on track, and what can I do to reengage with that reality?

⸸ July 15

Could you do this for me, please?

Nudge

Just a gentle nudge to do one small thing for yourself today.
It could be just a deep breath, a moment of peace, or a grateful thought.
Just one.
Could you do this for me, please?
Thank you so much.

Ask Yourself This…

How can I prioritize a tiny act of self-kindness, even in a small way, sometime today?

⸸ July 16

Knowing this was just the beginning of a day worth living.

This Morning, Before The Rain
This morning, before the rain, I stood before you in awe.
Watching the clouds roll in and reflecting light in new ways,
all the while growing darker by the minute.

This morning, before the rain, I realized that if not for these clouds and the certainty of change on the horizon, this moment wouldn't be as complex, breathtaking, and full as it would be if all were clear.

So I'm thankful.

Thankful for the realization that life's deepest lessons reveal themselves in the contrast that happens when changes mix darkness with the light, and that there is always beauty to be found.

Ask Yourself This…
What challenging situation in my life right now might actually be adding depth and beauty to my story, even if I can't see it yet?

July 17

Right now, at this very moment, there is someone who needs to hear what you have to say.

Your Voice
You may think your voice is small and weak.

That you have nothing of value to say,
and if you did, nobody would listen anyway.

You may look at others in awe, hang on their every word,
and let their messages go straight to your heart without a second thought.

You may think you are just a person who's surviving,
tumbling through days in such inelegant ways it would make Grace look the other way (and maybe you are...).

But underneath it all is you in your humanity.
You in your acquired wisdom.
You, in the strength that had you get up today.
You, with a voice people need to hear.
Yes, *your voice.*

Right now, at this very moment, there is someone who desperately needs to hear what you have to say. Someone whose life could be changed for the better if you just took a breath, and spoke your truth.
And more likely than not—*that person is you.*

Ask Yourself This…
Isn't it about time I overcame my self-doubt and believed that my words can positively impact others? And if I did, how would that change the way I see myself and live my life?

July 18

I can take this journey anytime I want.

Clouds
I sat in the yard.
Watching clouds go by—
Animals and Angels,
Warriors and Castles,
Ships on the sea, and tender smiles floating by.

And I started lamenting the fact I had somewhere to be,
when I realized that this dreamscape is here for me every single day.
That I can take this journey anytime I want.
All I have to do is be still, clear my mind,
and accept what is unfolding before me without expectation,
judgment, or precondition.

Then it hit me—despite all of our trying,
life works exactly the same way.

Ask Yourself This…
What is one small way I can add moments of stillness to my day, and more importantly, will I?

⳨ July 19

What we've forgotten.

Children
God gives us children to remind us of how strong we are,
how deeply we can love,
and most importantly, what we've forgotten.

Ask Yourself This…
What deeper parts of myself have the children in my life revealed, and how can I use this to prove to myself how strong, loving, and even innocent I can be?

⸸ July 20

...discover what living life on the edge really looks like.

Flip of a coin
On the Heads Up side is the productive you.
The one who shows up every day and does the things that need doing.

Heads Down is the quiet, reflective you.
The one who's at peace and ready to follow the calling of your soul at a moment's notice.

In the ever-so-thin middle is where the magic lives
that perfect balance of productivity and peace.

Heads up or down can work for a while, but standing perfectly balanced on the edge? That's where it's really at.

So are you living heads up, heads down, or balanced on the edge?

Take some time to think about it, and start to discover what living life on the edge *really* looks like.

Ask Yourself This...
What is one thing I can do to start discovering my ever-so-thin middle and more importantly, start to live in the magic?

July 21

You keep shining light because it's all you know how to do.

Black Holes
Some people are like black holes—
They carry their own gravitational force,
pulling light from every corner into their blackness,
and crush every dream you have to give.

They are both an empath's worst nightmare and greatest teacher of all—absorbing every last bit of your energy, while demanding you find a way to stay balanced on their edges if you're to survive

Maybe they were born this way.
Maybe it's depression, or something else out of their control.
Maybe within their depths beats a tender heart filled with enough love to withstand a force from which even light can't escape.

You keep trying because you believe that.
You keep shining light because it's all you know how to do.
And you keep holding on to the edge, in hopes that someday you'll be able to fill that hole, and see some light coming back at you from the other side.

If this sounds familiar, please be sure to take care of yourself.
Protect your energy, and above all, know when it's time to walk away.
Because your happiness, and so much more, depends on it.

Ask Yourself This…
Is there a black hole in my life right now that I should consider walking away from, and if so, what does that look like?

⸸ July 22

You are an unstoppable force.

You

You were born to do great things, and have everything you need
to achieve them—
the vision to see where you're headed,
the determination to keep yourself on course,
and the faith to sustain you when the road gets dark.
All there, waiting to be unleashed.

You are here to make an impact, be an instrument of change,
and better the lives of those around you.
And while you already have (some in ways you'll never know or understand),
you've always felt there's something bigger you're supposed to do.

So if you haven't started the practice of self-reflection needed to bring that to the surface—It starts now.

Ask Yourself This…

What small step can I take today to be more reflective, allowing the clarity I need to surface?

July 23

That thing you were supposed to be, do, or say is wondering why you've waited so long.

That Thing
I know you feel it.
That *thing* you were meant to be, do, or say that's still inside you.
The one that speaks so loudly, it makes you wonder if all "you" are is the way it gets around.

You know, the one you've never been able to bring to life and release to the world.

That *thing* is now asking what you're afraid of, and it spends most of its time hoping you'll realize it doesn't need to be perfect, it just needs to be seen.

So please take that leap of faith.
Try, fall, learn, rise, and try again.
That's what life is all about, and what your *thing* is calling you to do.

Is that *thing* speaking a bit more loudly now that you've read this? Is it begging for the chance to see the light of day, breathe, grow, change, and yes, even fail?

If it is, please honor its request.
Because what a tragedy it would be if your *thing* got so old,
it turned into regret and died before it could even take a single breath.

So, on behalf of your *thing*, I'm asking you to take one tiny step toward bringing it into the world today. Just one tiny step.
Please?

Ask Yourself This…

What “thing” inside me is waiting to be shared with the world, and more importantly, what tiny step can I take today to bring it to life?

⸸ July 24

It's just that you don't understand why you should have to…

Empath
It's hard being wired this way—
nothing hidden, heart unprotected, soul in full view for all to see.

But you're not weak. In fact, you're very good at protecting your interests, loved ones, and such.
It's just that you never understood why you should *have* to.

So you go forward, trying to navigate a heartless world from a love-filled place. And it drains you mentally, emotionally, even physically.

But you push through the days. Not only seeing others for who they are, but also understanding that look in their eye. The one that says they need the hug they don't know how to ask for. The one that you so badly want to give, but worry it's something they're not ready to receive, and hold back because your actions are many times not interpreted as intended.

Yes, it's hard being wired this way, but it's also a beautiful existence. It's living life on a deeper, more connected level than anyone can imagine; Always seeing the good in others, causing unexpected smiles, tears, and "I love you's"—and yes, even giving and getting that much-needed hug.

And I'm guessing that even if you were given the chance, you know deep down, that you wouldn't change a thing.

Ask Yourself This…
How can I remind myself to balance being an empath with maintaining my well-being, and in what ways can I do this?

⸸ July 25

...you only have this one moment.

Today Is...
My 91-year-old dad had taken a bad fall and found himself in the hospital. In his room, there was a dry erase board that read, "Today is July 25, 2023, You're in the hospital."

For me, that board represented more than just a reminder of aging and illness; it struck me as a reflection of our collective "Daily Dementia"—a testament to our constant busyness and distractions that often make it difficult to stay present and remember even what day it is.

Too often, we find ourselves living in the future, anticipating and preparing for what's next, or stuck in the recent past, replaying events in our minds.

So today, I want to share this reminder:
You only have this one moment, so please, slow down, take a breath, and appreciate the day.

Ask Yourself This...
How am I feeling right now, what blessings do I have, and—what is today's date? (See what I did there?)

⸸ July 26

...you've never once noticed when it's raining (and it actually rains a lot).

Sprinklers

You turn on automatically with your incessant Tick, Tick, Tick, Tick,
Doing your best to keep your little piece of the world green, growing, and yes, looking perfect. Trying ever so hard to hit that last blade of grass on the very edge of your property.
You can't have a brown spot now, can you?
What would people think?
That maybe you're not what you're pretending to be?
That when it comes to doing the important things, you just don't have what it takes? No, you can't have that.

So you turn on—
Same time, day after day.
Same pattern you've been using for years.
Same result, year after year.

Not as good as the yard next door,
but definitely better than the one up the street.
Day after day.

Tick, Tick, Tick, Tick.
Lamenting that the water pressure is low.
Tick, Tick, Tick, Tick.
Complaining that the sun is too high.
Tick, Tick, Tick, Tick.
Frustrated that your effort is unappreciated—
even by the flowerbed that soaks in your work because it just happens to be in the way.
Tick, Tick, Tick, Tick, Tick, Tick, Tick, Tick.

You're so caught up in the feeling your world would become a wasteland if you shut off for even a second, that you've never once noticed when it's raining—
and it actually rains a lot.

You've never accepted that the green nature intended for you
means you have no gears to grind,
no pressure to worry about,
no angles to calculate,
and no hoses to repair.

None.

All you have to do is sit back, let it happen,
and watch the grass do what it will.
Try this, and I'm sure you'll be pleasantly surprised at what happens when you just let go, and let nature do its thing.

NOTE: I'm not talking about inactivity; I'm talking about control and your addiction to it. So by all means keep the water flowing, but just be aware that there's an entire sky filled with it, just waiting to take your lawn to the next level.

Ask Yourself This…
What would happen if I allowed myself to let go of control and trust the process of growth in my life?

July 27

Every single one of us feels unprepared...

You're Wrong
I know you've been doubting yourself.
Thinking you don't have what it takes to reach where you want to go.
You feel like you're letting everyone down (including yourself),
and this bothers you—sometimes more than you think you can stand.
I've been there, I know.

But the truth is you're *not* failing or letting anyone down,
and you *do* have what it takes to get where you want and need to go.

How am I so sure?
Because you've survived every single day up to this point,
And you will survive this one (and another, and another, and another).

The truth is our mirrors only reflect flaws, not beauty, and *every single one of us sometimes feels unprepared* to take on what life throws at us.
This causes us to live with the belief we are both flawed and unprepared.

So take a breath. No, take *10 breaths*. In and out. Slowly.

Bring to mind all the things you've accomplished,
and all the challenges you've overcome.
Then look into that mirror and truly see yourself—
not as the unprepared, overwhelmed shell of what you think you should be,
But as the badass warrior you *truly are*.

Ask Yourself This...

When will I finally accept, once and for all, that I'm prepared to take on whatever life has to throw at me?

⸸ July 28

...do this, and you'll be amazed at what happens next.

If You're Happy (and You Know It)
When are you at your happiest?
What are you doing?
Who are you with?
What time of year is it?
Is it morning, afternoon, or night?
Keep reflecting and get specific.
Now ask yourself: Why?
Why do these things bring you such joy?
What is it about these people, places, activities, and times that elevates your mood, energizes you, and gives you hope?

Now think about how—
How do you bring as much of this into your life as possible?
How do you arrange your life to be in those places, with those people, and doing those things?
After doing this, you'll find connections that will provide clarity about yourself, and perhaps even illuminate a path forward.

Now do the opposite.
When are you at your unhappiest?
What are you doing?
Who are you with?
What time of year is it?
Is it morning, afternoon, or night?
Again, get specific.

Now ask yourself: why?
Why do these things bring you down so much?
What is it about these people, places, activities, and times that lower your mood, sap your energy, and make you want to give up?
Now think about how.

How do you remove as much of those experiences as possible?
How do you avoid those places, people, and activities?

You might feel a sense of relief just considering this, but you may also feel stressed, as these elements are part of a larger pattern that you've accepted for a long time.

Now be intentional.
Stay focused on bringing in the good and removing the bad.
Make it a practice.

It won't happen overnight, but do this consistently,
and you'll be amazed at how your life unfolds.

Ask Yourself This…

This piece was already filled with questions for you to answer. You're good!

July 29

Launching is one thing, but staying in orbit is really where it's at.

Forcing It
You've come a long way,
And now you're achieving things you once thought impossible.
I know—
You want to do more, be more,
and expand as quickly as you can.

That's great, but whatever you do during this time of growth—
Don't force it.

You know what I'm talking about
Being able to say "Yes" to everything that once seemed out of reach.
It feels amazing in the moment, doesn't it?

But trust me, the weight of *maintaining* what comes next
can bring you right back to where you started—or worse.

So don't chase yesterday's dreams just because you can.
And don't pursue new goals that don't align with your true path.
Launching is one thing
But staying in orbit is really where it's at.

Ask Yourself This...
What are my true goals during this time of growth, and what can I do right now to ensure I stay focused on them as my energy continues to rise?

⸸ July 30

Life has its way of balancing itself.

Blessings

Do you ever notice that most blessings are mixed with a bit of struggle, while others are disguised as heartache, loss, or even tragedy?
And both make you wait far too long to see the gift they truly are?

It's frustrating.

You don't understand why they have to come with so much work.
You can't comprehend why so much loss is required for your life to move in the right direction.

And it's hard to feel grateful for something that disrupted your life in so many ways and caused you so much pain—and maybe you feel a little guilty for feeling that way.

But life has its way of balancing itself out.
There's always a bit of good with the bad and bad with the good.
Day and night.
Sun and rain.
Birth and death.
Chaos and calm.
It's all there, all the time—pendulum swinging, darkness giving way to light, and back again.

So next time you find yourself frustrated that your blessings came with unwelcome pieces, or wishing you didn't have to suffer so much to accept the gift, stop and be grateful that in the end, there was far more light, than darkness.

Ask Yourself This…

How can I remind myself that "bad" and "good" are subjective when it comes to blessings, and to expect a little of each in everything that comes my way?

July 31

No, advice isn't what you need.

Anything But Normal
You sit back and watch the parade of normal people living normal lives, achieving normal milestones, and enjoying normal moments.
The way you always envisioned your life would be.

But it isn't.

Whether through fear or fate, sickness or sadness, yours is anything but.
And it bothers you, even though you tell yourself it shouldn't.
You try to look past it, but you know you can't.
Even though you know you have the power to rise above it.

Here's the part where I could say things like
"Comparison is the thief of joy,"
"The people you see are fighting their own invisible battles,"
and "Gratitude for your own life is the answer."

And while all of these are true, none of them help you when you're mourning the loss of the life you envisioned but never had.

No, advice isn't what you need.
It's empathy and a deep understanding of the ache you feel.
Because it's real, it's deep, and it's not easily solved.

So all I can do is stand beside you as the parade of normal passes by,
and try to help you look beyond the last hill—to see the beauty, wonder,
and magnificence that surely exists, in your own version of "normal."

Ask Yourself This
How can I let go of the vision of "normal" that I had for myself and instead embrace the life unfolding in front of me?

⸸ August 1

All it ever takes is time.

Annoyances
It's the little things.
The endless stream of what shouldn't be.
And the small roadblocks in your day.

It's being put on hold before you finish your sentence.
Constantly creating new passwords, and being surrounded on the road by people who somehow forgot how to drive.

It's those things that trip you up, derail your mindset, and bring you to the negative in an instant. But aren't you supposed to stay in "the now", be present, and live with grace and gratitude?

This sounds great, but when "the now" consists of trying to accomplish something for 40 minutes that should take five, it's almost impossible to be anything but annoyed.

So when those things are happening, *don't stay in the now.*

Time travel to the future in your mind, when the "thing" is done.
When you're off the road, your password is reset, or when you've talked to the person you've been holding for. Live in *that* moment for a second or two, avoid the daily tragedy of unnecessary stress, anger, and disruption, then have faith that that moment will come eventually. Because it always does.
All it ever takes is time.

Ask Yourself This...
How can I develop this habit and time travel the next time I start to get annoyed?

August 2

Coming back to the surface takes time.

From the Depths
You made it through, but maybe you don't have it all figured out yet—
why it happened, what you could've done differently,
and definitely not what things will look like moving forward.

But you think you've made some headway, so of course, you should feel at least a little better, shouldn't you? Maybe not. (At least, not right now.)

Maybe you need a few days (or even more)—to release everything that's built up inside from going so deep into stress, upheaval, and uncertainty, holding that heightened awareness, and cycling through emotional intensity for as long as you did.

It's natural.
It should be expected.
And it's okay.

Coming back to the surface takes time.
It's giving yourself the grace to rise slowly and being okay with that.
It means emotional rest, mental clarity, and letting go of the tightness that's still gripping your body. You're allowed to feel what you feel and when you feel it.

It doesn't matter what was said last, what agreement was made, or whether you were right or wrong. You're a human being with emotions, a nervous system, and a mind—all of which were affected by something that pulled you into a place you'd rather not have been.

So rise slowly if you need to, and in that gentle rise, remember: the people around you might need some grace too.

Ask Yourself This…
How can I show myself and those around me Grace as I heal?

♆ August 3

This is one of the dead ends of life.

Rejection—A Hard Truth
You want what you want,
when you want it,
from whom you want it from,
and on your terms.
We all do.

But most times, that isn't happening, and you have to accept that.

These are the bitter pills of life.
The soft and hard rejections from the people you most want acceptance from—and it hurts.

Especially when the one person you want to care simply doesn't.

This isn't one where I have an answer or even perspective.
This is one of the dead ends of life.
One where you simply have to find a path to acceptance.

You can't make someone care, appreciate, be attracted to, or even simply acknowledge what you so very much want them to.

Life just doesn't work that way, and the faster you accept that truth,
the better off you will be.
It's just the truth.

Ask Yourself This…
When will I shift my focus towards self-acceptance and away from seeking validation from others?

⸸ August 4

...your decision to start in the first place was valid in the moment.

Decisions
You've made the decision to read this.
Maybe it's a good one, maybe not.
Maybe it will move you, or it will turn out to be an utter waste of time.
But your decision to start in the first place was valid in the moment
just like the one you just made to keep your eyes taking in these words.
Both based on where you are now, how you're feeling, and every bit of experience from your past.

It's all you ever have to work with when deciding what to do in the moment, which is why regret for making any decision is one of life's small tragedies.

You can certainly lament the outcome, but the decision you made in the moment? Well, that was the *very best* you were capable of then.

I know accepting that can be hard, especially when things don't turn out the way you wished—but please try.
Because you deserve all the grace you can get
Especially from yourself.

Ask Yourself This...
How can I trust that every decision I make is the best I can do with the information and emotions I have at the time?

⸸ August 5

...keep only what serves you best.

Junk Drawer
Over time, life can start to feel like that junk drawer in your kitchen—full of things you have no use for, but keep around "just in case".

It's a jumbled mess that has you shuffling things around to see what's actually useful, and you swear that someday you'll get around to cleaning it out.

So isn't it about time you finally let go of those rarely used and broken things, and use that drawer for what serves you best instead?
Just sayin'.

Ask Yourself This...
What parts of my life am I holding onto that no longer serve me (people, things, habits, mindsets), and how would letting go and making space for what truly matters make a difference in my days?

⸸ August 6

The kind of hug you feel for days.

A Hug
If I were there,
I'd give you a hug.
Not a "side hug,"
a quick hug,
or a "nice to see you" hug.

But a real hug.

The kind that wraps you up and lets you know you're loved,
cherished, appreciated, and missed.
A hug that lingers—
one you can feel for days after,
warming you in ways that are hard to put into words.

That's the hug I'd give you.

But since I can't be there right now,
I wanted to write this instead—
to let you know that I'm thinking of you,
that I appreciate you,
and to send a little of the warmth
I'd give you if we were together.

(And if you can, take that warmth
and pass it along to someone else—
someone who might need a hug just as much as you do right now).

Ask Yourself This…
Who do I know who could use a hug right now (including myself)?

⸸ August 7

...our problems are more similar than we think.

My Problems vs. Your Problems
My problems are close; yours are far away.
My problems feel heavy; yours seem light.
My problems are urgent; yours can wait.
My problems are confusing; yours are clear.
My problems feel overwhelming; yours seem solvable.

But maybe our problems are more similar than we think,
and we'd both be better off if we saw them as *our* problems,
and worked on solving them together.

Ask Yourself This...
Do I downplay the problems of others in relation to mine, and if so, how can I change that?

August 8

...get out your sledgehammer!

Mountains

Given enough time, patience, energy, tools, and support
you could turn a mountain into dust.

Life's problems work the same way.

So step back.
Find your crew.
Get out your sledgehammer.
And begin.

You've got this.

Ask Yourself This...

How can I approach my problems with a mindset of patience and persistence, knowing that progress *is* possible with time, effort, and help?

⸸ August 9

Is this truly something I need to overcome?

Barriers vs. Guardrails

Some things that look like barriers,
actually turn out to be guardrails.
They might appear to be blocking your path,
but often, they're just there to guide you—
keeping you away from danger
as you navigate life's twists and turns.

So before you rush to break through,
step back and ask:
"Is this actually something I need to overcome,
or has it been put in my path to steer me
in a better direction?"

The answer to this question can be life-changing.

Ask Yourself This...

The next time I'm struggling with an obstacle, how will I remember to pause long enough to figure out if it's a barrier or a guardrail?

⸸ August 10

Communication is incredibly complex.

Outer Shell, Inner Reality
You think you talk too much (or maybe even that you're too quiet), and when you leave a conversation, people may believe you were inappropriate, tone-deaf, boring, self-centered, or even rude.

The conversation seemed fine, but later, when your mind had you alone, it replayed a much different version of what you thought happened.

So you start to overthink, regret, and wonder how you could ever be so blind to what was going on around you. You promise yourself you'll do better next time; You'll be mindful of your words, remember how badly you messed up before, and vow not to make the same mistakes again.

But you're missing something very important.

Your mind didn't include everything that was happening at the time. You no longer feel the energy of acceptance around you, or have the context, body language, and the incredibly complex natural feedback loop you were in at the time.

Social situations are hard to read, and perceptions after the fact are virtually impossible to get right. So take a breath. Because what you think was a disaster, was probably never given a second thought.

So give yourself permission to be yourself in front of others. Accept that you won't always say the perfect thing, and remember that who you are is beautiful, what you say matters, and people truly do like you.
You just have to believe it and let yourself be seen.

Ask Yourself This…
What can I do today to boost my confidence so I am more comfortable being myself without fear of judgment or overthinking?

⸸ August 11

Shouldn't you be sending as much Love as you can to where it needs to go most?

Love is a Choice
Love is a choice you make.
It's not something you fall into,
and it doesn't happen by accident.
You have to be open to it,
want more of it in your life,
and be willing to spread it to others.

Love—
that indescribable feeling,
the deepest of all emotions,
the purest and most perfect experience you can have.

So why do you hold even the smallest bit of it back?
Why do you reserve it for only those you think "deserve" it?
Shouldn't you be sending as much love as possible to where it's needed most?

This is one of the hardest things you can attempt:
To give your love to those whose actions have made them seem unlovable, to forgive the unforgivable, and to accept the unacceptable.

As impossible as it may seem, if you simply dropped your snap judgments and unrealistic expectations, and focused on spreading love as far, wide, and deeply as you can, I'm pretty sure you'd find yourself with a lot more to love.

Ask Yourself This…
Am I spreading love the way it's meant to be spread, freely and without condition? If not, why?

August 12

Seeing the good in others but none in your own mirror.

Self-Hatred
Seeing yourself as undeserving of love.
Recognizing the good in others but failing to see it in yourself.
And twisting your reality into something unrecognizable to others.
It keeps you small, hidden, disconnected from joy, and emotionally unavailable, even to yourself.

This cycle can feel inescapable, leading you to question your worth, purpose, and even existence. And you start wondering if a way to escape what you hear in your own mind even exists, because it feels so big and overwhelming.

I could talk about self-love right now, urging you to nurture the same love you give to the world back into yourself. That would be the expected—and probably the right thing to do. But I know that if you're reading this from a place of self-hatred, that message is likely one you're not ready to hear, because you're just not there yet, and that's OK.

All I can tell you for sure is that it begins with a faint flicker of awareness that all humans distort their reality to some extent, but all possess an undeniable inner beauty—one that may take some time to uncover, but is undoubtedly there. Yes, even you.

So start there. Take that first tentative step of simply accepting the fact that you are not alone in this, and that you, like everyone else, deserves love— especially from yourself. It's up to you to believe that, and make the decision to take the tiny first step to get there. And I truly hope you do.

Ask Yourself This...
What is one tiny thing I like about myself, and how many more can I find?

⸸ August 13

Your battery is dangerously low.

Low Power Mode
Warning!
Your battery is dangerously low.
Continuing on with your current settings may cause you to lose data, cause damage to your system, or shut down unexpectedly.
To avoid a critical disruption, please recharge immediately, or enter Low Power Mode.

There, I figured I'd write this one in a way that I know usually causes you to stop and take immediate action.

If you can do it for your phone,
you can do it for your body, mind, and soul.
Because neither of us want you to shut down unexpectedly, now do we?

Ask Yourself This…
Is it time I took myself offline for a bit to reset my operating system?

⸸ August 14

Connecting everything I am, feel, and think through the immutable power of love.

Centered Heart

My heart is centered,
sitting right where it should be, in the middle of it all—
connecting everything I am, feel, and think
through the immutable power of love.
The love I was born with,
the love I was meant to share,
the love that lies dormant in so many others,
just waiting for its chance to expand.
Just like it has for me.

Perhaps, with time, their love will too center,
surface, and break free into the world to do what it does best:
make disparate hearts one,
bring light where none exists,
and open eyes to the wonders of what happens,
when one simply takes a breath,
and lets it unfold.

Ask Yourself This…

What barriers or fears keep me from expressing my love in a more expansive way, and how can I overcome them?

⸸ August 15

A reality that is still here for you after what seems like an eternity away.

Waking from a Nightmare
You're on the other side now.
Your eyes open, focusing on the world as you wonder:
"What is real and what is not?"

Your racing heart and frantic mind—
remnants from a time you were living a nightmare,
untethered from the reality you now find yourself returning to.
A reality still here for you, after what seems like an eternity away.
It's different, yes, but still familiar and better than before.

So you lie there, trying to sort it all out—
what it meant,
where it came from,
and why, even now, you still can't seem to fully let it go.

Maybe tonight you'll finally find rest, now that hope has found the strength to break through. And maybe tomorrow, you'll be one step closer to freeing yourself from the nightmare, once and for all.

Ask Yourself This…
What parts of my past traumas are still present in my current reality, and what can I do today to start letting them go?

⸸ August 16

It will take a level of faith you don't yet understand.

Ready

Nothing will happen until you're truly ready.
If you try before you're ready,
progress will inevitably slow,
then come to a halt,
and you will surely stumble.
Momentum (if you can call it that) will become fleeting at best.

But when you're ready?

Things will just start to happen.
You'll awake with a drive that seemingly came out of nowhere.
And the doing of things that once seemed nearly impossible,
will simply become what you do.

This is the power of being ready.

There's no big secret to readiness, because it happens naturally when the discomfort from the contrast you feel between the life you want and your current reality is greater than what it will take to get you there.

So keep moving towards your goals.
Be consistent and get focused on what you want,
and you will be ready sooner than you think.

Ask Yourself This…

What small step can I take toward my goal today to start me on my journey to being truly ready to change?

⸸ August 17

Step further into the light that's rightfully yours.

Stepping Into Light

Most times, there is no real darkness to speak of—
nothing that rises to the level of tragedy or despair.
Most times, life just is.
It's in these quiet, ordinary moments—
when your mind is clear, stress is manageable, and you have good energy, that you have the clearest chance to step into the light of awareness.

Awareness of the life you truly want,
how you'd like to live it,
and who you want to share it with.

So the next time you find yourself thinking how ordinary the day is and you're struggling to think of something to do, take that as your cue to step into the light. Because what you find there might just turn that ordinary day into one that changes your life..

Ask Yourself This…

Today, how can I shift my perspective to see those ordinary moments as opportunities to go deeper within, even for just a second?

August 18

...maybe, you're just looking at it wrong.

Spiral

You're tired of this cycle.
Up, down, higher up, farther down.
"I'll never go there again," you say—
only to find yourself back the very next day.

You're tired of being tired.
Tired of making the same mistakes.
Tired of never feeling like you're on solid ground.
Just tired of it all.

And you start to wonder why.

Why all this "returning to"?
Why is there never just one clear direction?
Why does every step up seem to be followed by two steps back?
What is there to learn in this?
What's the point of this seemingly circular track?

But maybe you're looking at it wrong.
Maybe you're seeing it as flat,
when life is clearly three-dimensional.
Maybe that circle is really ascending all the time.
Maybe those steps forward and back
are really part of a spiral staircase.
And the reason you're so tired
is because you've been climbing higher and higher with each and every step,
and the only direction you've been heading—
is up.

Ask Yourself This...

Can I accept that every move "forward" and "back" are both just part of the same learning, and that life truly is a spiral after all?

⸸ August 19

A faith that I can't explain, but just know.

Keep Going
I can tell you lots of reasons why you should keep going.
But if you've already given up, then they probably won't mean much.

I can tell you who to keep going for if not yourself.
And I can tell you how much you bring to the world,
and the impact you've already made on so many others.

But again, if you've already given up, none of that will matter.

And that's where it gets tricky.
That's where I have to start talking about faith, and love, and the things that have no logical explanation.
That's where I just have to ask you to trust me and keep going.
It's in these moments that I'm scared.
I'm scared because I'm approaching your hard facts with my soft heart.
I'm looking into your cold eyes with warm intent, in hopes that what made them so cold will somehow start to melt.

Yes, I'm having faith in these moments too.
A faith that I can't explain but just know,
and I'm praying with all that I have
that it will somehow find its way in
and tell you in ways I simply cannot,
to just keep going.

Ask Yourself This…
What mindset shift do I need to fully rely on faith when things seem impossible, for either myself or someone I love?

August 20

...take life up on its standing offer.

Try Again
In every day
every hour
and yes, even every moment,
there is a chance to try again.
No failure is absolute.
No effort is ever in vain.
No time spent trying is ever wasted.
It's all more experience for you to draw on to make the next one better.

So please, if you feel like you've failed,
Do whatever you can to put it quickly behind you
and take life up on its standing offer—
for the chance to try again.

Ask Yourself This...
What can I do in a moment of "failure" to redefine it as learning, and quickly try again?

⸸ August 21

This isn't a time for "trying."

This is War
There's no other way to say it.
This is war.
A war for your happiness.
A war for your success.
A war for you getting to where you want to be.

This isn't a time for "trying", backing down,
or even giving an inch—
because your enemy never will.

The enemy that's flanked you 24/7 your entire life,
the one with great intel, that knows your weaknesses inside and out,
and is always waiting to go in for the kill.
Fear.

But here's what Fear hasn't seen while it's had the upper hand—
the desire burning inside you to become the person you were meant to be.

Your desire is stronger than Fear could ever be,
because it's coming from a part of you deeper than it can go—
it's coming from your soul.

So the waiting is over, and there are no more excuses.
Because when your true desire to change is combined
with the pure power and knowing of your soul,
Fear simply doesn't stand a chance.

Ask Yourself This...
What is one thing I can do today to start to understand how Fear is trying to keep me from the growth I desire?

August 22

The love I've poured into this is now yours.

Wherever You Are

I was almost asleep when something inside me gently stirred—
the need to connect with you in this moment,
because I sensed you might be feeling alone right now.

So I got out of bed just before midnight to tell you
that no matter when you're reading this—
whether it's days, years, or even decades after it was written,
that you are not alone.

I'm right here.
Giving you all I have in this moment
to bring you comfort,
lessen your burden,
and to let you know that my faith in you is so powerful,
I'd like to believe it brought you here right at the moment
when you may need it most.

The love I've poured into this is now yours.
And it doesn't matter where you are, what you're doing,
or the shape you're in.

In this moment, please know—our hearts are beating as one.

Ask Yourself This…

Am I open to the idea that there's a shared connection among us all that knows no bounds, including space and time?

⸸ August 23

You're Ok.
You're not alone.
You're going to get through this.
It's going to be fine.

Ask Yourself This…
What can I do to take a wider view of my problems to see that things always work out eventually?

August 24

Yes, I'm talking to you.

Wrong Places
I hate to say this, but your lack of confidence is showing,
and it doesn't look good on you—
especially when it's avoidable, born from self-doubt
and negative self-talk.

Yes, I'm talking to you, sitting in that chair,
looking for answers in every place but yourself,
taking way too long to find a shortcut to success
or a partner who will magically bring you along for the ride.

I think it's time you took a breath,
and once and for all, have that talk with yourself—
the one you've been avoiding for so long.
The one where you're honest about your strengths,
abilities, and true place in the world.

The one that starts in your soul and ends in your mirror,
where you finally see yourself as the incredible human being you are.

It shouldn't have taken me to bring you here, but that's why I wrote this—because I knew that if I didn't, you might still be sitting there, looking for answers, in all the wrong places.

Ask Yourself This...
What if the answers I seek are already within me, waiting for me to recognize, accept, and put them into action?
(Spoiler Alert: They Are)

⸸ August 25

There's something about the moments of first light.

5am

The world feels different at 5am.
Gentler, kinder
speaking in whispers, not shouts.
Whether quiet lakes or city streets
There's something about the moments of first light
That let you believe
Everything will be alright.

Ask Yourself This…

Can I start to get up earlier once in a while to experience the peace and inspiration that first light brings?

August 26

I can only be here for such a very short time.

When Kids Grow Up
I can only take you so far.
I can only give you so much.
I can only be here for such a very short time,
and I think that time is coming to an end (or at least changing).
Because I know that what I have to give is no longer what you need, and that we both have to accept the fact that our relationship has evolved into something different—
Me, no longer the provider, protector, and arbiter of what is right.
You, stepping into your own truth, making your own mistakes,
and learning the hard, unfiltered lessons that come with living.

I can only take you so far,
but I will never leave you,
and will *always* be here when you need me.
That will never, ever change.

Ask Yourself This…
How will we maintain a good relationship as it evolves into something new?

⸸ August 27

Imperfection is not failure.

There Are No Perfect Things
There are no perfect things.
Everything has a flaw.
Every person has work to do.
Everything can be improved.

And that's great news for you.

Because if you accept this truth,
you'll stop trying to be perfect,
create perfect things, and live a perfect life.
Then maybe you'll start to embrace the beauty in imperfection,
and see the nuance, texture, and yes, even joy that emerges
when you can simply appreciate what you've created
as it is.

Imperfection is not failure.
Imperfection is life itself.
So please, stop trying to be perfect
and simply live.

Ask Yourself This…
How does my obsession with perfection get in the way of my appreciation of the imperfect aspects of myself and others?

⸸ August 28

...tomorrow you will show up as you always have.

When It's Just You
People are well-intentioned.
They send thoughts and prayers,
and sometimes show up in ways you'd never expect.
And you appreciate all of it.

But deep down, you know that at the end of the day,
it's just you—you who will have to get your mind around it
and lower your expectations just to stay sane.
You who will show up tomorrow on an empty tank,
inching uphill like you have for way too long.

Just you.

So be thankful for those who care.
Internalize the positivity and well-wishes coming your way,
and try to use some of it to fill your tank.

Because tomorrow, you will show up, as you always have.
doing what needs doing,
making the decisions that need to be made,
and moving yourself—and those you care about—
a little closer to not needing thoughts, prayers, or well-wishes anymore.

You may not like it, but you're uniquely built for this.
And even though at the end of the day, it's just you,
you know deep down that you have more than enough
to make it through.

Ask Yourself This...
Knowing it's just me that has to navigate what I'm going through alone, in what ways can I take care of myself so that my tank never truly runs dry?

⸸ August 29

This is how we share our true worth.

True Worth
Kindness, love, and purpose.
Deep conversations over simple meals.
Time spent creating, learning, and connecting.
This is how we share our true worth.

How much more connected we become,
when we measure each other not by what we've earned,
but by what we've learned and how much we've grown.

How much better we serve our children,
when we teach them not just to earn more,
but to love more deeply,
seek understanding over accumulation,
and find joy in small moments.

This is how we create a world where people awake
everyday not from a dream,
but into one.

Ask Yourself This…
What can I do to show my true worth to others and create the opening for them to do the same?

August 30

That thing you've been holding on to.

Release
What do you need to release?
Is it joy, fear, love, hate, creativity, guilt, inspiration,
or negative thoughts?

What is it?

That thing you've been holding on to,
the one you've pushed deep down and kept hidden—
the one that occupies so much of your mind,
that it's slowly burning its way to the surface.

That one.

Well, it's time.
Time to finally release its stranglehold on you,
or to bring it joyfully into the world for all to see.

Whichever it is, it needs to happen—
and now.

Ask Yourself This…
What have I been failing to release into the world, whether positive or negative, and how has it impacted my overall well-being?

⸸ August 31

Looking for the lesson in hardships is an act of faith.

Hard Lessons

What is the struggle you face that always seems to resurface?
The thing that, no matter how hard you try, never seems to go away?
Well, whatever it is, it's trying to tell you something—
something you haven't been able to hear but desperately need to learn.
Because you've focused more on the pain it's brought
than on the lesson that came with it.

This is one of life's hardest challenges:
To separate yourself from what you're going through
enough to understand what's happening below the surface.

But it's necessary.

Looking for the lesson in hardships is an act of faith,
and in those times when you can no longer comprehend
what is happening or why, faith is what you need most.

So the next time you find yourself exasperated while fighting the same battles you have before, stop, wonder, and ask:
"What is really going on here, and what am I supposed to learn?"

This shift in perspective might not only be what you need in the moment but will ultimately set you free.

Ask Yourself This…

What things do I seem to struggle with constantly, and what do I think they are trying to teach me?

⸸ September 1

The most accurate personality test is your reaction when someone says, “You can't do that.” So, what type are you?

Ask Yourself This…
When I hear someone say, "You can't do that," how do I typically react? What thoughts or emotions arise within me?

⸸ September 2

Just because you're taking on water does not mean you're sinking.

Progress Isn't Linear

If life were fair, progress would be linear. But it isn't.
How frustrating, right? You're moving forward, when BOOM!—upheaval hits you like a torpedo you never saw coming.

Now here you are...
Water rushing in, alarms going off, and panic setting in.
And despite all the hard work you've put in, you're back where you started—or worse, sunken lower than before.

Damn.

But here's the thing
Just because you're taking on water doesn't mean you're sinking.
It just means that maybe part of your hull wasn't quite strong enough for the deeper waters ahead. And even though it's probably a blessing in disguise, it can derail you if you let it.

That's why I wrote this. To remind you to have the presence of mind to step back, detach from the emotional whirlwind, and see it for what it is—a process. You will find yourself in this situation again and again, wondering why things went wrong when everything seemed so right. And then you will learn and grow—every time.

So accept the jagged line of progress for what it is—the most challenging but quickest path from where you are now, to where you so badly want to be.

Ask Yourself This...

How can I remind myself that setbacks are not signs of failure but part of the process of getting stronger and closer to my ultimate goal?

⸸ September 3

That is the wisdom conceived in struggle and birthed in awareness.

The Beauty of Pain
The brightest light is shown on our strengths and weaknesses when we're struggling. It's when we learn, grow, resist, evolve, and hopefully, go deep into ourselves to discover what truly is.

That is the beauty of pain.

That is the wisdom conceived in struggle and birthed in awareness
That is the lesson life keeps trying to teach us again and again,
with faith that one day,
we just might understand.

Ask Yourself This…
Do I accept the premise that "The brightest light is shown on our strengths and weaknesses when we're struggling"?
Why or why not?

⸸ September 4

...there are also these things called boundaries, rest, priorities, and focus.

So Much
I know—
You want to do everything, try new things,
go to new places, and meet new people.
You want to show up for those you love
help out in your community,
and be there whenever and however you're needed.
And that's really great.

But there are also these things called
Boundaries,
Rest,
Priorities,
and Focus.

These are the things that will keep you
On track,
Sane,
Happy,
and Productive.

So if you want to do everything,
start with those four.
I promise that if you do,
everything else will come to you faster
than you could ever imagine.

Ask Yourself This...
How will I resist the appeal of doing everything all the time all at once long enough to focus on setting boundaries, resting, setting priorities, and focusing on what's most important?

⸸ September 5

You might be surprised at what you hear.

Checking In
I felt the need to check in on you,
because something seems off.
Not terrible, or even bad—
just... different.

Maybe I'm imagining it,
or misinterpreting the feeling.
But it was strong enough to make me want to write this.

This slight unease.
This "not exactly right."

So if you're feeling like this,
promise me you'll take some time to breathe into it,
because it might mean something dormant is about to surface,
or even that the incredible thing you've been holding back,
is ready for the world to see.

Please stop and take some deep breaths,
clear your mind, and listen to what your heart is saying.
Because you might be surprised,
by what you hear.

Ask Yourself This…
Do I have "that feeling," and if so, will I ignore it, or honor it with some thoughtful time and reflection?

⸸ September 6

What could have been the purpose?

Wonder

Do you ever wonder if you just "came to be",
or if you had a say in this before you were born?
Were you given the option to stay in perpetual bliss,
or to become human and experience all that life has to give?

If you were, then you know what you chose.
But that begs the question: Why would your higher self choose to give it all up to be in your particular body at this exact time and right in the place you find yourself now?
What could have been the purpose?
What could have been going on in the netherworld
that led you to make the absolutely insane decision to become who you are now?

Maybe you should take a moment to reflect on that and ask your higher self for some insight.
Because who knows,
they just might be willing to share.

Ask Yourself This…

What are the things about my life that are so amazing that I would've given up the chance at perpetual bliss to experience?

♱ September 7

You know there are struggles behind every smiling face you see.

Brave

How brave you are—
stepping out into such a massive and unpredictable world
with your heart on your sleeve to face whatever comes your way.

This world—
unrelenting, unforgiving,
And full of unexpected twists and turns.
Filled with people all trying to protect their own hearts,
but never showing even a hint of vulnerability.
And that makes you wonder:
"Is it just me who is struggling just to make it through the day?"

But deep down, you know you're not alone.
You understand there is pain and insecurity behind every smiling face, and that, like you, most are still searching for something just beyond their reach. They're just better at hiding it.

Yet despite it all, there you go,
still walking out the door every day with your heart on your sleeve,
into a world where hearts are rarely seen,
and smiles seldom returned.

How brave you are.

Ask Yourself This...

Do I give myself credit for how brave I am, even though it may seem I'm anything but?

September 8

Stop looking for quick fixes.

Switches and Dials

When it comes to change, I know you prefer instant results over gradual adjustments—like a switch. One flip. Instant happiness.

But life doesn't work that way.
Real change isn't made by flipping switches,
but more like turning dials—ones in need of constant calibration.
A little to the left, a little to the right.
It works for a while, but not forever.

You know this. So why are you still surprised when the mental switch you flip doesn't work? (again). More importantly, how do you break this pattern you've been stuck in for so long?

It all comes down to stopping and starting.
Stopping the search for quick fixes, setting unrealistic expectations for yourself, and thinking sustainable change comes from a single decision.

Then *start* focusing on where you want to be, adjusting each dial in your life carefully and intentionally. Focus on this daily, and eventually you'll see that you've shifted your direction completely.

This isn't just about habits, it's about awareness. It's about consciously dialing in your thoughts, actions, words, media consumption, and the people around you. Each a factor in determining where you end up, and how long it takes to get there.

Ask Yourself This...

What switches have I been trying to flip? And which dials need adjusting to make real change happen?

⸸ September 9

...maybe you should start thinking about your life's purpose instead.

Life's Purpose
You've spent a lot of time trying to figure out your "life's purpose"—that one thing you were sent here to do.

That singular focus you see in people who seem to spend every waking moment moving in one direction, toward one goal, and in service of one result. And you wonder, *will I ever find mine?*

I think the question you need to ask yourself instead is, *What do I truly care about?*

That is where purpose lies, in the things that bring you into flow, make time stop, and make you want to be better. So start by identifying those things, then follow the thread outward to see where they go.
And you might just find your purpose along the way.

Ask Yourself This...
What keeps pulling me back, even when it's difficult? And what would happen if I actually followed that instead of managing around it?

⸸ September 10

... it could also be your soul trying to tell you something.

It's 2:53am. (Yes, written at 2:53 am.)
Why is it that in the middle of the night, you often find yourself awake and uncomfortable?

Is it leftover stress that was never released?
Negative thoughts that were never resolved?
Or perhaps a dream that strayed too close to the surface to remain in its own world?

It could be any of these.
But maybe it's your soul trying to tell you something, and the middle of the night is the only time you're quiet enough for it to be heard.

Usually, you meet being awake at this hour with annoyance.
You try desperately to get back to sleep, your mind already time-traveling to the moment when your alarm will unleash the weight of the day's expectations—ones you'll now be too tired to meet (or at least meet well).
I get it.

But in that frustration, you might be missing an opportunity:
The chance to be still with yourself, in silence, *simply listening*.

A tall order for sure, especially if your muscles aren't exactly cooperating. But your soul keeps no time but its own, waits for the chance to connect with you, and simply asks that you listen.

So, do yourself a favor—the next time it happens, take a breath, be still, and make the effort to hear what it's trying to tell you.
Because what it has to say, just might change everything.

Ask Yourself This...
What might my soul be trying to tell me in the quiet moments I usually overlook?

September 11

Are you trying to simply fill the small crevices in your life while ignoring the large gaps?

Wants and Needs
Do you find yourself *needing* what you *want,*
yet *not wanting* what you *need*?

Are you attempting to fill the small crevices in your life,
while ignoring the larger gaps that really need filling?

This is an important question to reflect on, as it brings into focus so many aspects of how you're running your life, what you value right now, and how you're spending your time.

So my hope for you is that you to get to the point
where you really *need* to get what you *need,*
and just *want* to get what you *want.*
Now go fill those gaps!

Ask Yourself This...
What are the gaps in my life that really need filling, and isn't it about time I prioritize this over simply getting what I want?

⸸ September 12

You need time, and I need connection.

Time and Connection
I know you need time.
Time to heal, process, and make yourself as whole as you can be at this moment. I know I need to feel connected to you. To know you're ok, safe, and in a place from which you feel you can rise.

Both of us are doing our best to get through this moment
to find that space in the middle—the space where both our needs are met, and we can find what will pass for peace right now.

This is difficult.
This is stretching.
and sometimes feels unbearable.
But I know by going through this,
we are both growing, learning, and
coming to terms with the hand life has dealt.

You need time, and I need connection.
But we both need each other.
So it's a good thing that the love holding us together is infinitely stronger than the force trying so hard to pull us apart.

Ask Yourself This…
During hard times with someone I love, how can I remind myself to focus on the love that underlies the connection to allow for the time necessary for healing and growth?

⸸ September 13

...ask just once.

God Needs a Minute
You're praying for something—something important and essential. Maybe for the health of someone you love, your finances to turn around, or even just the sense of peace that you haven't felt in so long.
So you pray every day.

You barter, make deals, and swear you'll be better. "If I could just get this one thing, I won't ever ask for anything else again... Promise."
But the next day nothing happens. And you pray again. A month later, nothing's changed. So you keep praying. Eventually anger sets in.
You feel ignored, even hopeless, and start to wonder if God exists at all.

But what you failed to realize in all your anger and disappointment is that God doesn't work in the "flash of light" miracles you were expecting. Rarely is there a quick resolution to big life challenges, even on a divine level. Yes, even God needs time to get things done. It takes time to set into motion the millions of actions, circumstances, and people that will lead to you getting what you want.

So instead of asking for the same thing everyday, ask just once, have faith that you were heard, and then simply be grateful that it's being worked on. Pray not for what you want, but in gratitude for the effort God is making to get it to you.

So have faith, live in gratitude,
and be patient and ready to accept what God has prepared for you.
Because while it may not be exactly what you want,
it will always be what you need.

Ask Yourself This...
How can I trust the gradual unfolding of life, recognizing that divine timing will usually not align with my own expectations?

⸸ September 14

Irrationally, it felt like it would never stop.

The Rain (A True Story)
The wind whipped and the rain pelted my window,
changing tone and pitch throughout the night.
Doing its best to sound like voices or animals howling in the distance.
In my half-awake state, it felt like it would never stop, and the sky would never clear.

Then, in the height of my annoyance, I had a thought—"Surrender."

So I cracked open the window and braced for the chaos of the night
to do what it would. But as the once ferocious storm met my willing acceptance, there was a shift.

The midsummer shower that exhaustion had turned into a fearsome beast now revealed a softer side.

Without resistance, the storm simply became white noise,
and gently lulled me into a dream.

Ask Yourself This…
When will I finally accept the storms that blow through my life, knowing that within them lies the potential for growth, transformation, and inner peace?

September 15

These motivations drive you, determine your actions, and literally shape your life.

What are You Missing?
You're always looking for something aren't you?
Always trying to fill the voids in your life,
searching for the someones or somethings
you think will make you whole.

And this drives you.
Shaping the way you show up in life.
Determining what you do, how you behave, and the way you navigate the world.

And it can be maddening.

So maybe it's time to slow down,
think about the voids you're trying to fill,
and trace them back to when they became so important to you.

The answers you uncover there,
might just be the ones you've been searching for your entire life.

Ask Yourself This…
What deeper emotional needs or desires have I been trying to fill, and how can I create more self-awareness to truly understand what I need?

⸸ September 16

The tiny, more accessible dreams that you can make happen at any time.

Thimble List
You know your bucket list—
The trips, experiences, and "once in a lifetime" events
that will happen "someday."
But what's on your Thimble List?
The tiny, more accessible dreams that you can make happen anytime?

If you don't have a Thimble List, maybe it's time to make one.
Make it long and deep.
Fill it with things that fill you up and slow you down.
Then one by one, start doing them and crossing them off.

And maybe when you're done,
you'll realize that the things on your bucket list
really weren't that important after all.

Ask Yourself This...
How can I prioritize and make time for the smaller things that bring me joy and fulfillment?

September 17

Passion and Purpose are dependent upon each other.

Passion vs Purpose
Passion can be surface. Burning bright for a time, showing itself in ways that are easy to see, feel, touch, and experience. But it's also dependent on the continuous spark of clarity or inspiration from something deeper within.

Purpose is what remains after the fire of passion burns down.
The smoldering embers that stay hot and hidden deep beneath the surface, keeping alive what burned so bright.
Purpose, then, is the distilled version of what you were so passionate about.

Passion and Purpose are dependent upon each other.
Passion is the expression of the feeling purpose creates.
Purpose is the driving force behind it all.

So what are you passionate about?
And could it be strong enough
to become the purpose that gets you out of bed everyday?

Ask Yourself This...
What am I *truly* passionate about, and could that actually be my purpose after all?

⸸ September 18

So take a breath, and just be present.

When You Can't Help

The title of this could've been "Helpless," because that's exactly how you feel when all you want is to ease someone else's pain but can't. Yet, despite how it feels, you're not truly "helpless." "Help" is subjective, and your version of it might just not be what they need at that moment.

So you have to ask yourself, "Who am I really trying to help here?" Or "What am I really trying to accomplish with all my heart, energy, softness, strength, and effort?" It may not make sense to say to yourself, but if what you're doing isn't working, continuing down that path is ultimately for your benefit, not theirs.

I know, sitting in silence and watching someone you love twist in pain is one of the hardest things you can do. But sometimes it's the *only* thing that can be done in the moment.

So take a breath, and just be present with them.
Sit in silence and try to understand what brought them to this place.
Then let them know that they are loved, supported and will never ever have to go it alone.

Ask Yourself This…

How can I remember to accept that just by just being present, I am helping someone in pain?

⸸ September 19

...accept those things that make you unique.

You're Not Special
You're definitely *unique*,
but in no way are you *special.*
There's nothing that will exempt you from the trials of life,
and you don't deserve anything extra for just being you.

But if you play your cards right,
your uniqueness will be more than enough
to bring you places being special ever could.

So look in the mirror and find those things that make you the unique,
one-of-a-kind masterpiece you truly are.
Because you don't need to be special, to lead a *very* special life.

Ask Yourself This...
What are the things that make me a unique one-of-a-kind masterpiece?

⸸ September 20

...just focus on the things that will get you through the next minute, hour, or day.

The Should's

You should:
lose weight,
eat healthier,
exercise more,
stop your negative thoughts,
be a better friend,
learn a new language,
and *finally* purge the basement.
Yes, you *should*

But what if you simply *can't* right now?

What if life has thrown you curve after curve, and you're just too busy, too tired, and maybe even too depressed from picking yourself up off the ground to do the things you "should"?

Well, I guess you simply shouldn't then—and instead, show yourself some compassion and grace.

Just because something is the right thing to do, doesn't mean you have to do it right this minute.

So please, stop "shoulding" yourself into oblivion, and instead, focus on the things that will get you through the next minute, hour, or day. Take a breath and congratulate yourself for what you accomplished instead of feeling guilty for what you didn't do.
Yeah, maybe that's what you should do, and that's ok.

Ask Yourself This...

Am I so focused on the "Shoulds" in life that I'm completely overlooking my state of being right now?

September 21

Moments and opportunities you'll never get back.

Grand Theft
I know you think you're aware, but are you really?
Because you're being robbed every single day.
And I'm not talking about a few dollars in hidden fees.

I'm talking about the *grand theft* of your time and attention by the thieves of doom scrolling and the mindless clicking on anything that looks remotely interesting.

I know you're tired and need a break, and that you just want to relax and enjoy some "downtime." But when that downtime stretches into hours instead of minutes, you've done more than just take a break.
You've surrendered precious moments you could have used for yourself—or even others—that you'll never get back.

I hope you not only remember this the next time you start to scroll, and protect your time and attention as the priceless things they truly are.

Ask Yourself This…
What can I do to remind myself to stop spending my time and attention on things that don't serve me?

⸸ September 22

Only one that's valid... (but not really)

Twenty-One Excuses
It's too hot.
It's too cold.
It's too rainy.
It's too humid.
It's too dark.
It's too early.
I'm too tired.
I'm too busy.
I'm too nervous.
I'm too clumsy.
I don't feel like it.
I don't have time.
I don't know how to get there.
I don't have good shoes.
I don't know anyone who's going.
I don't want to be sore.
I'm not good at it.
I'm not prepared.
I'm not in good enough shape.
I'm not in the mood.
There's bugs.
Twenty-one excuses not to go outside.
Only one that's valid… (but not really)
Just go outside and do something.
Please?

Ask Yourself This…
When will I make going outside everyday a priority in my life?

⸸ September 23

I'm so glad you're here.

Hey…
If you have a second,
I'd like to talk to you.
I like these moments.
Just you and me,
sitting here having a chat.
Just a moment or two to put life on hold and just focus on each other.
I think this is the way life is supposed to feel.
Safe, tuned in, and connected.
Do you agree?
(I'd imagine you do)

So really, I had nothing much to say today…
Other than that I appreciate your taking a minute
to slow down with me and just *be.*
So thank you.
I'm so glad you're here.

Ask Yourself This…
Who can I call or text today and invite for coffee or a chat?
(You know, that someone you haven't seen in forever that you really miss…)

⸸ September 24

...it's not really the way they look that's bothering you.

Appearances
When you see someone whose appearance makes you uncomfortable, recognize the fact that you are seeing a person who is having the courage to show their true self to the world.
And just maybe, it's not really the way they look that's bothering you, but the fact that you aren't doing the same.

Ask Yourself This...
What is holding me back from showing my authentic self to the world, and what would happen if I did?

⸸ September 25

It's a cycle I don't think we're even aware of.

Pressure and Space

The world is so compressed right now.
In everywhere you go, and with everything you do—
whether online or offline—
there's pressure.
Pressure to do more, buy more, be more, go farther, move faster, and pay closer attention. Pressure to be ready to move up in line, GO the instant the light changes to green, and NEVER make a mistake.

You feel it, right?
That pressure is baked into virtually every part of every day, the kind of pressure that seems unavoidable no matter how hard you try.

Well, here's the thing: Everyone else feels it too. And because of that, we're all causing and receiving it all the time. And it's a cycle we may not even be aware of.

It just is.

So, instead of continually adding to it. What if you focused on giving others more space? Space to think, breathe, and move, and yes, even to make mistakes.

Think about how your own life would change if you made the commitment to both seek more space for yourself while giving more to others.

What an unexpected gift you'd be giving and what a better life it would be, if you just took a breath, and let others take one as well.

Ask Yourself This…

Am I ready to remove myself from the constant cycle of pressure in the world, and be a creator of space instead?

⸸ September 26

A light so pure and powerful that it couldn't be denied.

Your Life, Your Light
You've done your best to live a life you could look back on with pride. Trying hard to make the right decisions at the right times, and sharing your heart only with those who would treat it with care.

But these things didn't always work out the way you thought they would. In fact, it seemed that more often than not, you were left wondering how things that felt so right could possibly go so wrong, constantly trying, failing, trusting, hurting, finding, and losing.

And you wondered if it would ever change, then started to think it wouldn't, almost accepting that your trying would never be enough.

But deep down, you knew that your life would one day, work out for the best.
So each time you fell, you got up, tended to your wounds, and tried again.

And now here you are—older, wiser, harder, softer, centered, resilient, and strong. You've proven that success isn't absolute. That everything brings both unexpected consequences and silver linings, and the very things you've been regretting for so long have turned out to be the very foundation of your happiness.

This is a good time for you. You're not so concerned with making the right choice every time, and you're not looking back with regret.

For the first time, you're simply trusting yourself and moving forward with a strong mind, open heart, and trusting soul.

Ask Yourself This…
Looking back, what are the pivotal moments you can identify in your growth, and how did they build upon each other to bring you to where you are today?

September 27

What are the "must today" parts of your life?

Not Today
Sometimes you wake up and think, "Not today."
You don't have the energy for the effort.
You can't find a way to motivate yourself to move.
No, not today.

And you tell yourself that's okay.

Maybe today is the day you need to reset. Maybe not doing today will set you up for tomorrow. Maybe there's a reason you don't have it in you today.

And that's all well and good, but there's a problem.

You have responsibilities and commitments. You have things that must be done, no matter how you're feeling.

"Not today" doesn't work for the "must today" parts of your life.
So, what do you do?

Today reverse-prioritize. Make a list of what you *don't* have to do, freeing yourself from those things, and doing your best to get through the shortest versions of what needs to be done. Then, say "not today" to your heart's desire.

Ask Yourself This...
What are the "must today" parts of your life, and how can you consistently hyper-prioritize them to allow time for the rest you need?

⸸ September 28

...our time together is special and will never be taken for granted.

The Honor of Your Time

What an honor it is to have your attention right now.

It means so much to me that you would spend some of the precious minutes of your life reading what I've written for you. Seriously.

With the world pulling for every bit of your attention, it's not lost on me that our time together is special. So today, I'm going to use it to remind you of some of the reasons you're so deserving of the attention the world is trying so hard to get from you.

First, you're beautiful. Yes, you are. How you define "beauty" is up to you, but I challenge you to look into your own eyes in the mirror. In those eyes, you'll see not only the physical beauty of color and contrast, but a lifetime of learning, heart, joy, sorrow, and strength.

Next, you're worthy. Worthy not only of the attention you receive, but of all the things you desire. You were born worthy, and will remain worthy until your last breath.

Lastly, I believe in you. Most likely we've never met, but I truly do believe in you. Why? Because if you're still reading this, I know you've made commitments to yourself that you're honoring right now. Yes, right now you are moving forward, and I simply know that you can and will keep going.

So thank you again for the honor of your time. Believe that you are truly beautiful, worthy, and on the right track. Because that's the truth, and deep down, you know it.

Ask Yourself This...
How can I strengthen my belief in my own worthiness and appreciate my beauty beyond just physical appearance?

⸸ September 29

...it's in this gap that most dreams die.

The Curse of Clarity
I have to warn you that the clarity you're seeking actually comes with a curse—the curse of contrast.

It's the gap between what you now know is your destination and where you find yourself right now. It can be maddening seeing how "off" things are for the very first time, knowing how far you've strayed, or how different the world is from what it's meant to be—so be prepared.

Understand that this awakening you've just experienced will eventually bring joy, but traversing this gap will be difficult at best.
I know it's not what you want to hear right now,
and it's definitely not in line with how happy you thought you'd be when you discovered the life of your dreams.

But it's in this gap that most dreams die.
It's where life gets hard and sometimes overwhelming,
and you start to wonder if you'll ever find the other side—
the side that shines so bright now that you have clarity.
Such an amazing thing, but one whose dark side is rarely discussed or ever planned for.

So please take care.
Do your best to find clarity,
but know that it is in this contrast that the journey truly begins.

Ask Yourself This...
How did the line "But it's in this gap that most dreams die" make me feel, and how do I plan to navigate these gaps?

September 30

Maybe we all need to stop taking things at face value.

LOOK HERE!
Look over here! No, here!
Hey you! Look at THIS!!
Can you believe he said that? Click HERE!
Watch out for that!

FEAR! PAIN! CURIOSITY! WONDER! TRAGEDY! DESPAIR!

And there you are, just trying to get through the day without being distracted, sold to, lied to, torn down, pulled away, or pushed aside.

It's a confusing world we live in, isn't it?

Maybe it's time to stop taking things at face value, start questioning the motivations behind what you see, and most importantly, the effect it's having on your happiness.

At this point, you can't simply "turn it off" and function in today's world, so maybe understanding it and turning it down will have to do.

Ask Yourself This…
How can I stay aware of the underlying motivations of the things that are pulling at my time to keep myself above their influence and maintain my level of positivity?

⸸ October 1

So leave the outward exploration for another day.

Telescopes and Microscopes
When looking at life, it's better to use a microscope than a telescope.
Telescopes can bring wonder and amazement, for sure,
but they also surface questions like, "Why am I here?"
"Am I significant?" and "Does my life even matter?"

Microscopes, on the other hand, reveal that even in the smallest and seemingly insignificant parts of life, there exists purpose, meaning, and a natural need to move and grow.

Seeing this makes you realize that if such vast, interconnected complexity can exist in a tiny piece of grass, what potential there must be for a life as advanced as yours.

So leave the outward exploration for another day and get microscopic.
You'll be amazed at just how much you find when you take a breath
and see how incredible your life truly is
on even the smallest level.

Ask Yourself This…
When will I start to truly appreciate the small, meaningful details in my life, and what is one thing I can do today to start?

⸸ October 2

I think it's time for you to be self(ish).

Who Do You Think You're Talking To?
Why the negative self-talk, second-guessing,
building up of others, and tearing yourself down?

I think It's time for you to finally accept that you're no different than anyone else and that the people you talk to all have the same insecurities, fears, and need to be accepted and loved.

And you can prove it to yourself by just being observant. Notice how people fidget before speaking, pause mid-sentence to gauge reactions, or laugh a little too loud when nervous. This can be liberating.

Once you see that everyone's struggling with the same doubts you are,
it might be a good idea to take a good hard look in the mirror,
straighten your back, and step into the power you've had all along.

Ask Yourself This...
Isn't it about time I realized everyone struggles, and how much my negative self-talk is holding me back?

October 3

...maybe it's time for you to step back.

Growth
You're frustrated but looking forward.
Scared but hopeful, alive and truly living.
Every minute seemingly accounted for,
yet so many are slipping away.

It feels exhausting, exhilarating, and you want it to stop,
yet you're insanely curious about what's next.

You feel underprepared, overwhelmed, incapable, masterful, intelligent, and ready to lead at any given moment. All the while wishing someone would just show up with a detailed roadmap for you to follow.

The highs seem heaven-sent, the lows spine-snapping, instant, and seemingly inescapable. And this leaves you feeling like you can't keep this up, and that a breaking point is fast approaching.
So what do you do in this chaos of growth?

You Stop—
Stop planning, wondering, regretting, anticipating, thinking anything is "definite" or "impossible", and most importantly, expecting.

Yes, stop it all.

Because in this period, everything is in flux, and you need every bit of your focus and energy just to keep taking those small steps forward.

So stop, look, listen, and instead of making plans, accept that you're on the move, and ride the wave to wherever it leads.

Ask Yourself This...
Am I trying too hard to step into this period of growth, and would I be better served being more open to what will be without expectation?

⸸ October 4

Warm, happy, and free.

Create the Space
You need to create a space just for yourself—
To heal, wonder, and breathe.
To cherish who you are and love yourself deeply.
To get quiet and listen to what your heart has to say.

So make this space and this time for yourself—
Soft, centered, and light,
warm, happy, and free.
Hidden from everyone but you.
It could be a room, a park bench, or even somewhere in your mind
Wherever it is, make it a priority.
Then protect it with everything you've got.

Because we all need a place we can go,
to be ourselves, free ourselves,
and release what the world tries so hard to make us hold.

Ask Yourself This…
What physical space can I create that is mine alone, and what can I do today to start claiming it?

⸸ October 5

...maybe it's time you cracked the lid a bit.

Simmering pots

Underneath our lids, we're all simmering.
Some at a slow boil, others steaming and ready to spill over.
But the lid always stays on, keeping a sense of order on the stovetop, containing what we've decided is meant to be served later.
But the thing about lids is that while they're fine when things are warm or even hot, they're all but useless when the simmer turns to a full boil.

Now, I don't know if you're cool, simmering, or ready to spill over, but wherever you're at, maybe it's time to crack the lid a bit, show others what's cooking, and make sure the meal actually gets served.

Because I'm sure what you're cooking up for the world,
is absolutely delectable.

Ask Yourself This...

What am I holding back, and what small step can I take today to start sharing it?

⸸ October 6

It's in the letting go that it comes together.

Hold on for a Minute
Stop here and take a breath.
Don't think about your troubles
or how your problems will be solved.

Just stop, breathe, & relax.

You don't have to say or do anything in this moment.
You don't owe anyone an explanation or justification of how you came to be here, or why you've chosen to stay this long.

Just hold on.

Because it's in moments like these that solutions appear.
It's in the letting go that it all comes together.

Believe that.

Because your solution is inside you right now—
just waiting for you to get quiet enough,
for it to be heard.

Ask Yourself This…
What can I do today to begin the practice of pausing long enough for my soul to begin speaking?

⸸ October 7

I think our future looks bright.

Business
Whether you know it or not, we're all in the business of reshaping the world into a better place. Sounds like a big undertaking, doesn't it? Like a Fortune 100 kind of thing, with boards of directors, massive corporate funding, and business suits—*lots* of suits.

But changing the world is actually the smallest business there is.
It's a mom-and-pop, brother-sister-friend kind of thing.

A collection of "Soul Proprietorships," all moving in similar directions with the same intent—to simply do the small things every day to make life better for the people around you, with the hope that over time, it spreads further and further into the world.

Sounds cool, right?

So it's nice to be in business with you, partner.
I think our future looks bright!

Ask Yourself This…
What can I do *today* to make a positive difference in someone's life?

⸸ October 8

I'll just try my best to keep you quiet.

Oh, You Silly Mind

So there you go again…
Up in the middle of the night, chattering away,
Looking for danger in safety and trouble in paradise.
You silly, silly mind.

And I find myself wishing that the heart knew how to speak,
or the soul was more assertive—
then, my silly friend, you'd finally be put in your place.

But for now, I guess I'm stuck with you—
enduring your negative self-talk,
dealing with your drama,
and finding a way to make it through the day
with you narrating it in the worst of ways.

So I'll just do my best to keep you thinking positive thoughts,
creating some distance between your "reality" and the truth,
and gently encourage the passion of my heart and the knowing of my soul to take their *rightful* place.
Which is, of course, *Top of Mind.*

Ask Yourself This…

How can I quiet the mind and create moments of stillness to hear the whispers of my heart and soul?

⸸ October 9

This simple daily practice can be life-changing.

Let me guess
If you're not "doing," you feel like you're "lazy."
If you're not "busy," you feel like you're "failing."
Maybe you look at others who are always on the move and think "Wow, they're really going places," or "Their life is *so* much more interesting than mine."

You think you must be missing something and wonder why there isn't more happening for you.
And maybe this stirs up feelings of lack, envy, and shame.
Or sometimes, the opposite takes hold, and you find yourself inspired, driven, and determined to bring your life "To the next level."

Well, I've found that overcoming these feelings all comes down to asking yourself "*How can I make this moment the absolute best it can be?*" Then doing whatever that is.

This simple daily practice can be life-changing, because it quickly refocuses your mind from what you lack to finding the extraordinary in the most ordinary of days. So I really hope you try this one!

Ask Yourself This...
How could you make *this* moment the absolute best it can be?

⸸ October 10

...*wanting* and *needing* are two different things.

I know nobody is coming, but…
Nobody is coming to save you. It's true.
But that doesn't mean it's wrong to want to be saved.
Wanting someone to show up, bear your burdens, and move you to a place of safety is natural and ok.

But *wanting* and *needing* are two different things.

Everybody wants to know they aren't alone in this world, and to be shown proof that they're loved, supported, and have someone there that will help them reach their goals. But *needing* that proof constantly is something else entirely.

Making your own happiness dependent on the actions, words, and even presence of others might bring you happiness for a short while, but in the long run? Not a chance. Because the odds of your needs perfectly aligning with another's time and capacity to support you are virtually nonexistent, and honestly, unhealthy at best.

So please, don't ever make yourself wrong for wanting for someone to show up and save you, and of course be grateful when they do. But if you ever find yourself thinking you need it to be happy, stop and ask yourself why. Your answer just might save yourself some time in the darkness.

Ask Yourself This...
Do I feel like I want or need support, and why? (Be honest now!)

⸸ October 11

"Thoughts and Prayers" can only go so far.

How Are You?
Lately, it seems that everywhere I look,
I see good people going through hard things.
And not just the regular "trials of life" kind of hard,
but the ones that make you wonder how people are finding the strength to navigate. And it breaks my heart.

So if you're going through something otherworldly,
and wondering where the strength will come from—
Know that right now, in this moment,
I'm thinking about you, sending love,
and keeping you as close to my heart as I can.

That said, I know that my "thoughts and prayers" can only go so far,
and the only person truly walking this path is you.
And this can feel especially lonely.

I get that, because I've felt the same way.
So please take this as a gentle suggestion to reach out to someone you trust and ask for help. Even if it's just for a minute to talk. If you're not comfortable with that, then the next time someone asks how you're doing, be just a little more honest in your answer.

Maybe by giving the love behind the *thoughts* the opportunity to take action, you'll help all those *prayers* break through and start on their way to being answered.

Ask Yourself This…
How can I open myself up to the love and support of others during difficult times? And how will my opening up give others the opportunity to show the love they so desperately want to give?

October 12

Give yourself the grace you deserve.

Giving Grace
I know you tend to beat yourself up over small things,
and that you probably speak to yourself in ways you'd never speak to anyone else.

So I wrote this for you this morning in hopes that the next time
one of those conversations starts to happen, you can stop, take a breath, and give yourself the grace you deserve.
Because you don't deserve to be spoken to like that.
Ever.

Ask Yourself This…
How can I remember to stop, take a breath, and give myself the grace I deserve when the negative self-talk starts?

⸸ October 13

Maybe it's time to redefine what a "fire" is.

FIRE!
You see fires every day.
Some are small and containable,
others raging out of control.
And many whose flames have been extinguished,
but are still smoldering hot enough to reignite with the slightest breath.

But just because something's on fire doesn't mean it's up to you to put it out. In fact, most can safely be left to burn out on their own.

So maybe it's time to redefine what a "fire" is in your life,
and promise yourself only to fight the ones worth fighting.

Ask Yourself This…
What beliefs have led me to feel responsible for putting out every fire I come across, and how can I challenge these beliefs to create healthier boundaries?

⸸ October 14

Love isn't a short-term solution; it's a lifelong plan.

Choose Love
When you're looking for answers, Love is always sitting quietly in the back of the room with its hand up, while others, like greed, judgement, anger, resentment, and frustration are jumping out of their seats waving for your attention.

But while you know that choosing Love is *always* the right thing to do, it isn't always the most satisfying choice now is it?

Why? *Because Love isn't a short-term solution, it's a lifelong plan,* one that is the hardest to stick to when your pain, frustration, and ability to remain calm is usually at its lowest.

So the next time you're looking for answers, pause, take a deep breath, and choose love first.
It may be the harder choice in the moment,
but it will always be the right one.
Every. Single. Time.

Ask Yourself This…
When I'm facing a difficult decision, how can I remember to look to the back of the room and choose love first?

October 15

No cracks left to deepen, weaken, and split.

River Stone

The jagged edges of your resistance—
the imperfections you call "flaws",
and the parts of you that resist the flow—
will all be worn down and polished by time and experience
into a beautiful river stone.

Nothing left for the current of life to catch.
No cracks to deepen, weaken, or split.
No part too high or too low.
And no change, whether the river rages or gently drifts by.

Just a feeling of contentment with where you are,
the wisdom of knowing the river never stops,
And accepting of the fact that resisting what it brings
will only keep you tumbling, painfully, downstream until you release
your need for control, and stop.

Ask Yourself This…
How can I release my resistance and willfully accept the lessons and growth that life inevitably brings?

⸸ October 16

These are the questions that matter now.

What is your dream?
Is it true to you,
or just what you've been told it should be?

Is it what you really want,
or a safe, unreachable fantasy?

Is it worth the effort to bring to life,
or not worthy of your time?
These are the questions that matter now.

Because time is always slipping away.
And even worthy dreams tend to slip with it.

So—
What is your dream?
Why is your dream?
How is your dream?

And most importantly
When is your dream?

Ask Yourself This…
Isn't it about time you made "*Someday*"
"*Today*"?

October 17

You have so much more to get and give.

Ok, Enough!
It's time to do whatever needs to be done to get where you want to be.
No BS. No using fear of failure as an excuse to stay where you are.
No pointing to past mistakes as reasons not to try again.
And no believing you only have one shot at what you want,
because every single second is another opportunity to start again.

So here's your wake-up call—
You have so much more to get and to give.
Enough waiting.
Enough excuses.
It's time.
Get up and get going.
You have the life you deserve just waiting for you to step into it.

Ask Yourself This…
What's one action I can take in the next 10 minutes to move closer to where I want to be?

⸸ October 18

The life-changing truth of simply being grateful for what you have...

Life Persists
Life is relentless in trying to teach you what you need to learn,
but the more you resist, the harder it becomes.
So to truly get what life has to give, you need to focus on a way of living that *celebrates peace* and is *centered in love.*

Now, before you write this off as overused hippy talk, hear me out...

I'm actually talking about strength, gentle power, and balance.
I'm urging you to return to some truths you may have pushed aside:
The truth of connecting your breath, heart, and soul through meditation, the transformation that comes from living in gratitude, and the undeniable reality that we are all deeply connected.

Yes, I think the discontent you feel is telling you that it's
finally time to quiet your mind and open your heart to what life is trying to teach you.

In the meantime, life will persist—
Until, of course, the day comes when you decide once and for all,
to simply stop resisting, and claim what is yours.

Ask Yourself This...
When will I make the decision to simplify my life, reconnect with its basic truths, and finally stop resisting?

⸸ October 19

The question isn't who will let you, but who can stop you.

Ask Yourself This…

Isn't it about time I stopped asking for permission and relentlessly pursued what I want in life?

⸸ October 20

What is that special thing?

That Special Thing
I want you to think about something you love about yourself.
What is it about you that makes you smile?
What is that special thing?
I'd love to know…

Ask Yourself This…
What are some things about me that bring a genuine smile to my face when I think about them?

October 21

...fully immersed, wondering what would happen next?

Theatre

You're the star of the show, right?
Nothing happens without you.
And like most people, you probably think you also have to be
the writer, producer, and key grip (whatever that is).

But what if the key is to also be in the audience?
Not disconnecting completely, but watching the entirety of what's happening instead of trying to control every moment?

Think about the last great movie you saw—
Remember how you felt during those twists and turns?
Edge of your seat, fully immersed, wondering what would happen next,
but also content to let it all unfold—and probably not wanting it to end.

Yet, no matter how sweet, dramatic, terrifying, hilarious, or
heartbreaking it was, you were able to watch, think, feel, and learn.

Do the same with life.

Show up and be truly involved in what's happening, but also make a practice of stepping back and watching the rest of the performance unfolding around you.

So continue acting, directing, producing, and "gripping" if you must, but always remember to sit in the seats once in a while,
and take it all in.

Ask Yourself This...

Am I spending so much time trying to play my role perfectly that I completely forget to step back and just watch the movie?

⸸ October 22

You wouldn't think life would be so simple, right?

Try
All you can do is try.
That's it.
Just get up, get moving, and give it your best shot.

You wouldn't think life could be so simple, right?
But if you just get out of your own way,
keep your expectations low,
and do your best every day—
It most certainly is.

Ask Yourself This…
What does "Do your best every day" mean to me, and how can I remind myself that my best is enough?

⸸ October 23

I know you're doing the best you can, and honestly, that's really all you can do.

Hard Times
You're going through a hard time and would love some support.
But "thoughts and prayers" aren't what you need right now, and who wants to be the one with the black cloud over their head anyway?
Not you.

So here you are, feeling alone, trying to process, accept, and overcome, all the while putting on a happy face for everyone but yourself.
And it's exhausting.
And I know you want to stop.

Well, all I can tell you is that you're not wrong for how you're handling things. You're doing the best you can for you, and honestly, that's all you can do.

So tomorrow, try to do one simple thing for yourself.
Then try to do it again and again.
It might take longer than you want it to, but someday, those simple things will amount to something meaningful in your life, and you'll find yourself in a better place than you are today. I'm sure of it.

So please, keep trying.

Ask Yourself This…
What will I do today to move?

October 24

Simple but intense focus on what needs to be done next.

Head Down

There are times in life when the opportunity to better yourself seems limitless, and you do in ways you never thought possible.

Then there are times when growth seems impossible. These call for a shift in how you see yourself and how you approach your journey,
And being fine with grinding through life inch by inch.

This can be especially tough if you're the kind of person who isn't used to keeping their head down and accepting slow progress over constant growth.

So in these times, it's crucial to show yourself grace, compassion, understanding, empathy, and Love, *lots* of Love.

But even those will only take you so far. The only way out is through
a simple but intense focus on what needs to be done next.
Tiny, methodical steps toward small, achievable goals.

Don't stop to feel sorry for where you are.
Don't look to the future.
And *do not* beat yourself up if some of your good habits fall away.
As long as you stay focused and keep moving inch by inch, all of those habits will return, and everything you dreamt about will once again feel within reach.

Ask Yourself This…

What's one small step I can take today to get back on track?

⸸ October 25

Maybe it's something you should at least think about.

About Your Job…
I just wanted to ask you something—
Do you think it might be time for you to quit your job and do something else?
Something more aligned with who you are and what you want to be?
Just asking....

Now if reading the above just caused a pang of anxiety,
then maybe it's something you should seriously think about.
Because it's probably time.

Ask Yourself This…
Is what I'm doing for work truly aligned with what I want to do with my life?

⸸ October 26

Let life in.

Moments to Remember
It's easy to let life play out unnoticed.
Task to task, moment to moment,
always thinking ahead to what needs to be done next,
not being present with what *is*.
Then suddenly, a day has passed,
then a week, a month, a year—
and you find yourself struggling to remember the last time you did something just for fun.

Sound familiar?

That's why I'm writing this. To remind you to be intentional about being present and staying in the moment.

So let life in.
Feel what it's offering you.
And be present enough to turn "ordinary" moments into ones you'll remember forever.

Maybe it's a walk in the woods,
a drive to watch the sunset,
or even just catching up with a friend you haven't connected with in a while. Whatever it is, find a special moment to appreciate.

Life is too short to let it slip by without truly enjoying what it has to offer. So please, open your eyes, and make it happen.

Ask Yourself This…
Have I fallen into the trap of seeing "busy" as a badge of honor? And if so, what can I do to change my perspective to value what truly matters?

October 27

...You only have one shot.

"The Feeling"
Sometimes, you can just *feel* the creative energy in you.
It's so strong, it feels like something that *needs* to break free and make its mark on the world.
You can't sleep.
Your mind races.
And it's 2 a.m., then 3, then 4...

You're trying desperately to rest,
yet hoping the feeling will still be there when you wake.
And you're torn between what you need to do in the morning,
and the inspiration you're feeling now.

It's in those moments you need to get out of bed and get to work.
Write down everything, even if it doesn't make sense.
Do whatever it takes to get it out, get it down, and make it real.

Because those moments come from a special place
and under incredibly rare circumstances.
They break through because you're at rest,
with your mind disengaged and open to what needs to flow.

So the next time your mind spins in the middle of the night—
Honor it. Make it real. And bring it to life.
Don't worry about being a bit tired in the morning.
You only have one shot.
So take it.

Ask Yourself This...
What will I keep by my bedside to capture inspiration when it strikes, and how will I honor what I capture in the morning?

⸸ October 28

Go just a little bit out of your way.

Do Something About It
When you see someone in need, don't just stand there or look away.
Do something about it.
Yes, it *is* up to you.

Because if you're reading this, I'm guessing you have a big heart and want to do better—not just for yourself, but for others.

So please, the next time you see an opportunity to help someone, go a little bit out of your way, and just do it.

Ask Yourself This...
How can I train myself to take immediate action when I see someone in need?

October 29

Maybe we can start celebrating our wins first.

Celebration

I used to have a bad habit.

When I accomplished something, instead of immediately celebrating the result, I focused on how it could have been better, feeling not the joy of completion, but the disappointment from the contrast between the result and my expectation of perfection.

This not only robbed me of a beautiful moment, but affected my level of overall happiness, making me wonder if I would ever get "there".

Sure, recognizing where things fall short is important, but making that the primary lens through which you view your work leads to nothing but disappointment. And even though I've been reminded of this countless times, the perfectionist in me tends to brush it off.

So, I'm hoping this little reminder will make both of us realize it's time to stop. And just maybe—we can start celebrating our wins *first*, and think about what could have been better *later*.

Ask Yourself This...

How can I strike that elusive balance between continually looking for ways to "improv" and genuinely celebrating my wins, both big and small?

⸸ October 30

...giving yourself too much grace can be dangerous.

Grace
When you're going through a hard time,
giving yourself grace is essential.
But there's a fine line between giving yourself grace
and giving up on your goals,
so it's crucial to know where it lies in your life.

Grace allows you to accept that you won't always have the drive, energy, or capacity to get to where you're going.
But *too much grace* can easily creep into the habit of putting off what you should do today until tomorrow, which eventually sabotages forward progress altogether.

So when you're going through a hard time, be sure to keep the bar raised—at least a little bit. Set your goals lower if you must, but don't you dare abandon them altogether in the name of "Grace."
Because if you do, the time you spend in that place you're trying so hard to escape could feel endless.

Ask Yourself This...
How can I remind myself to both give myself Grace, while still holding myself accountable when times get tough?

⸸ October 31

Simple things that happen to us, especially as children, take on lives of their own.

What is that thing that's holding you back?
Believe it or not, it's very likely coming from something that happened a long time ago, maybe even as a child. It's true that even the simplest things that caused us pain, upheaval, or confusion, especially as children, can take on lives of their own, causing our subconscious to do everything it can to avoid even the *possibility* of ever feeling that way again. So even though the event has long since passed, your defenses are still on high alert, simply because you've never taken the time to tell them they're no longer needed.

This can be heavy stuff, so it requires self-analysis and root cause work in which you objectively look at how you act, then trace it back to understand why. And most of the time, it takes a trained professional to guide you through it.

So if you're feeling an underlying sense of discontent and find yourself feeling "off" more often than not—I gently ask you to start being more reflective about what you're doing and how it's holding you back. And with that fresh in mind, find someone who can take you back, help you see where it all started, and release it once and for all.

Ask Yourself This…
What are some patterns or behaviors holding me back, and who can guide me in addressing the deeper factors that may be driving them?

⸸ November 1

... eventually, you'll find the light again.

Dark Rooms
Did you ever notice that when you walk from a bright to dark room, you can't see a thing at first?
Then, slowly, your eyes begin to adjust, and it transitions from dark to dim. Shapes begin to appear, and what seemed impossible to navigate just moments ago becomes somewhat clear. And you move forward.
Life works the same way.

When you're suddenly thrust into darkness, things may seem impossible. But with time and patience, obstacles will be put into perspective, your path will become clearer, and eventually,
You'll find a way out.

Ask Yourself This...
How can I cement the analogy of entering a dark room so that it is accessible to me when life gets challenging?

November 2

You're much more like "them" than you think.

Who do I think I am?

Seriously, I'm not one of *them.*

You know, the professionals and experts. The ones who were figuring it out while I was wasting time. I'm one of *us*—the ones who look at "them" and wonder why we "didn't think of that," only to quickly tell ourselves that we're simply not wired that way and never will be.

So after all the mistakes, missteps, and dead ends I've enthusiastically charged down, who am I to believe that my thoughts are valid enough to put myself out there as one of "them"? Ridiculous!

And I also know all of that is *complete BS.*

My life experience *does* make me uniquely qualified to share my thoughts (as does yours). The only thing that separates "*us*" from "*them*" is that when they feel like we do, and trust me, they do more often than you'd believe, *they find a way to ignore it and keep moving forward.*

It really is that simple—and my proof is right here in your hands.

So please, the next time you're feeling unworthy of attention and wondering where your tiny voice fits in a world of megaphones,

take a breath and remember that *you* have something *they* do not: Your life experience.

So start by taking an inventory of all you've overcome, because in there you will find your unique perspectives on overcoming hardship, moving forward, and getting back on track, then go ahead and prove that you're much more like "*them*" than you think.

Ask Yourself This…

What is one small way I can step into my power over the coming week?

⸸ November 3

...whatever it may be is sitting there, just below the surface.

Making Peace
There's probably something you've been holding on to that needs to be let go. Maybe it's someone from your past, something you did or that was done to you, or even a dream whose time has passed.

Whatever it is, it's just taking up valuable space, holding you back, and keeping you from getting what you deserve now.
It's also waiting to be released.

So maybe it's time to start doing the work.
Reflecting on what no longer serves you, accepting where it came from, why it needs to go, and finally opening up space for what should be there instead.

Ask Yourself This...
What is something from my past that I have been holding on to, and what will I do to make peace with this person, situation, or thought?

⸸ November 4

The things that will unfold from there will amaze you.

Change the World

If you're ever directly asked to help change the world
even in the smallest way—
just say yes.
The things that will unfold from there will amaze you.
Promise.

Ask Yourself This…

What holds me back from saying yes to chances that can make the world a better place, and what can I do to see them not as obligations but opportunities?

⸸ November 5

It's time for you to move inward.

Self(ish)
I think it's time for you to be a little self(ish).
To let the world do what it will, without your help or attention.

Now I'm not saying you should withdraw completely— that's not you. What I am saying is that I think it's time for you to *conserve some energy for yourself,* so you don't lose yourself in service to others.

So take this as a gentle nudge to be just a little self(ish) this week.
Because most certainly, you deserve it.

Ask Yourself This…
Isn't it about time I became a little more self(ish)? Just a little?

November 6

...you're blaming the size of your cup.

Only 12 ounces

If you overfill a cup, do you blame it for being too small,
or simply stop pouring when you realize it's spilling over?
Maybe how you view your own capacity should work the same way.

So next time you're beating yourself up for not being able to take on more, remember you're blaming the size of your cup, and simply focus on what you can let go of to keep it from overflowing.

Your capacity isn't a reflection on your work ethic, level of caring, or ability.
It's simply your capacity at this time.
So please stop making yourself wrong, and accept that.

Ask Yourself This...

When I start to overextend my capacity, do I blame myself or try to prioritize?

⸸ November 7

There's too much upside to find...

Complicated

Do you have a way of taking something simple
and turning it into something so complex
it's hard to explain—never mind understand?
Do you swear you want a simple life,
yet still go to great lengths to make things "the best they can be"?
With Every. Single. Thing?

Have you told yourself this needs to change?
That this time, you'll let the idea stay small,
only to complicate it all over again?

This isn't a flaw.
It's just you.

Because you're someone who sees upside where others don't,
and that's not a problem,
it's your gift.

So the next time you're turning something small
into something others can't imagine, stop and realize
that you were built for this; And that without people like you,
the world would not even come close to being
the best that it can be.

Ask Yourself This...

How can I balance my tendency to bring things to the next level (and beyond) with my desire to have simplicity in my life?

November 8

Choose one thing to let go.

Choices
That to-do list?
Those goals?
The things you "have" to do?

They might not feel like it,
but they're all choices you're making
in support of the life you've built.

But now, you're waking up stressed,
wondering if there will ever be time again "just for you."
Sound familiar?

So here's the question
What do you choose to *matter less*?
Not just in order of priority
but in value, purpose, or place in your life.
Because prioritization is *"the order in which,"*
while "matter less" is *"if at all."*

So try this—
choose only what makes sense for you to do now.
Then choose one thing to let go.

Just one. Then repeat.

Life is about choices, and each shapes your happiness in the moment.
But all of them over time?
That can make or break your life.
So please, choose wisely.

Ask Yourself This…
What in my life can I choose to "Matter Less" and let go?

⸸ November 9

Know that the dream will be up and at it again in no time.

It's ok to put your dream down for a nap…
Your dreams are like two-year-olds.
You love them more than anything,
but they require you to operate on a whole other level
just to keep them alive.

Dreams don't care how much you have to do in your "normal" life;
They just know you brought them into existence to thrive,
and they will demand every bit of your attention until they do.

But here's the thing: dreams, like children, can—and should—be put down for a nap once in a while. And the reasons are exactly the same: sometimes you just need the break, and the dream needs time to let the work you've put in process.

So if you find yourself getting worn down from keeping that dream alive, take that break with no guilt, regret, or thoughts that you're giving up for good.

Accept that you need a break to reset, renew, and recharge,
and that the dream will be up and at it again in no time.

And when it is, you'll be ready to jump right in and help it grow
in the best way possible.

Ask Yourself This…
How can I create a healthy balance between pursuing my dreams and taking breaks to rest and recharge?

November 10

...just keep leading with your heart.

Your Purpose Will Find You
What I've learned is that if you keep leading with your heart,
are open to experiencing the highest highs and lowest lows,
and *truly* expect things will just work out—
you will start living your purpose without ever being consciously aware of it.

Yes, your purpose *will find you*,
if you're patient enough to let it.

Ask Yourself This…
How does this perspective on finding my life's purpose feel to me?

⸸ November 11

Be sure to add some windows and a door as well.

Walls
You've been hurt.
It cut deep, and now you don't know if you can ever trust anyone again.

You just want to withdraw, build a wall, and stay hidden,
never giving anyone the opportunity ever again to make you feel the way you're feeling right now.

I get it.
And you know what?
Maybe you should.
Honor what you're feeling and take some time to heal without the worry of trust, confidence, and opening your heart to anyone.

But please, if you do decide to build that wall,
don't make it so high that you can't see over it.
And be sure to add some windows and a door as well,
because at some point in the future, you'll be ready to come out,
and what a shame it would be that when you did,
there was nobody left to greet you.

Ask Yourself This…
How can I protect myself while healing without shutting out those who truly care about me?

⸸ November 12

Watch them as they try to do their best and sometimes fail.

A Day in Their Life
Here's something that might help you understand someone better.

Find a quiet space and get centered.
Breathe slowly and let your thoughts settle without judging them.
Now bring someone you'd like to understand better to mind.
Just sit with the thought of them for a minute.
Try to release all judgment and the emotions that the thought of them brings up. For now, just see them as another human trying to make it through their day.

Now, as if watching a movie, start imagining what a full day for them is like.

Picture their interaction with you, strangers, friends, their family, and coworkers. See them navigating traffic, phone calls, and everyday frustrations.
Watch them as they try to do their best and sometimes fall short.

Now ask yourself what you saw that you hadn't considered before,
and how might this change how you interact with them?

Ask Yourself This…
What's one thing I observed about this person that could help me approach them with more understanding?

⸸ November 13

Be more efficient than you have to.

Stealing from Tomorrow
They say don't put off until tomorrow what you can get done today. Be more efficient than necessary, and squeeze every minute you have in service of your dreams, goals, and aspirations.

And they're right. Why?

Because life is unpredictable, and once you put something down, there's a possibility it will be a long time before you can pick it back up.

So don't take that chance.
Use the capacity, circumstances, and energy you have at this moment, regardless of how slight—to move forward.

If you make this a practice, you'll find that the things you once saw as impossible will somehow start happening.
And your life will change in ways you might find hard to understand.

Ask Yourself This…
How can I use the thought of the realization of my goals to maintain a sense of urgency to truly make the most of my days?

⸸ November 14

But with each tiny step, there'll be progress.

I'm ready
I'm ready to stand on my own two feet.
Build the life I want.
And learn the skills needed to make this happen.

I'm ready to wake up each morning with purpose,
choose growth over comfort, and invest in myself.

I know that fear will try to hold me back
by telling me I'm not ready, not smart enough,
and don't have what it takes.
But I won't accept that.

Instead, I'll value progress over perfection,
take small, actionable steps,
and have gratitude for it all.

This is a good time for me.
I'm ready to move.
And excited to become
the best version of myself
I've ever been.

It's been long enough.
No excuses.
Let's go.

Ask Yourself This…
What steps can I take today to move forward on my journey out of darkness? What support systems will I need to help me along the way?

⸸ November 15

Because they're in, all the way.

Your Rock
Who will be there when life gets serious and messy?
Who will never leave your side?
Who will never make you wonder if they'll be there tomorrow?
Who is all in, all the way, with no questions, hesitations, or regrets?

If someone comes to mind, reach out to them today.
Let them know how much they mean to you.
Tell them they're your rock.
And don't forget—*being* someone's rock is just as important as having one.

(And if no one comes to mind right now, that's okay too.
Sometimes our rocks aren't who we expect—
like a friend who showed up when it mattered, or even a family member we may have taken for granted. Think hard enough and you'll see that someone has always been there for you in some way.)

Ask Yourself This…
What does it mean to you to have someone who is "all in" without any questions or hesitations?

⸸ November 16

Hold the ones you love just a little longer.

Life's Fragility
You never know how long you have or where the road may lead.
You never know what the next moment will bring or if there are brighter things on the horizon. You just never know.

So all you can do is honor the moments you have with awareness.
Awareness of the joy or lesson they lead to.
Awareness of the "ordinary" ones that will someday feel special.
And awareness of how you're using them wisely,
or letting them slip away.

This has all been said before in many ways.
Anyone who's experienced significant loss might have written it.
But I did.

Not only for the losses I've already suffered, but for the ones I now see that are unavoidable, imminent, and already being processed.

So I used these moments to write this, hoping this rendition of "life's fragility" would stir you to stop for a moment, see the people in your life, and appreciate *what is*.

So please, cherish your moments.
Make a habit of holding the ones you love just a little longer,
and slow down to appreciate the moment,
That is now.

Ask Yourself This…
What would I do differently today if I truly believed each moment was precious?

⸸ November 17

So get off the hamster wheel for a bit.

It's OK to be OK
I think it's time for you to realize that sometimes that
"just ok" is good enough, and "average" is just fine.
It's time to be satisfied with satisfactory
and to walk—not run—in the direction of your dreams.

It's time to slow down.
Rest.
Coast.
Be easy with yourself.

Did you just feel the resistance rise up?
Did even considering that seem wrong?
If it did, then maybe you need to read it again, because you probably need to slow down more than you realize.

So step off the hamster wheel for a bit.
Make room in your day for yourself.
Pause. Rest. Recharge.
Smile, accept, and breathe.

Release that pressure to constantly achieve and just *be*—
at least for a little while.

It's ok to be "ok" for as long as you need to be.
Really, it is.

Ask Yourself This…
What would it feel like to give myself permission to be "just ok" today?

⸸ November 18

There are definitely brighter days ahead.

Above the Line

You're spending a lot of time looking down lately
down on yourself, your actions, and prospects for the future.
You're beating yourself up, tearing yourself down,
and keeping yourself decidedly below the line of "fine".

So I wish that you could see yourself through my eyes,
because then you would understand just how much you mean
to the world, and how much you have to give.
There has never been a single person on earth like you,
and there never will be again.
Your perspective, heart, soul, mind, and presence are gifts—
even though you can't see it right now.

Now maybe you don't believe that, and if so there's nothing I can say
to change how you feel about yourself.
But if you can at least be open enough to consider it,
that would be enough for now.

Yes, this might be a dark time for you,
and darkness has a way of making you believe that it's all there is.
But that's not true.

So keep going, even if it seems pointless.
Please keep trying, even if you feel success is impossible.
Please be as gentle and accepting with yourself as you are with others,
even if you feel you don't deserve it.
Because you certainly do, and there are definitely brighter days ahead.

Ask Yourself This…

Who can I connect with that will challenge my negative self-talk and help me find moments of light and hope during difficult times?

⸸ November 19

Yes, you can still live up to your highest ideals.

Capacity Does Not Equal Responsibility
Someone you care about needs something done.
Something you do well.
You have the time to do it, and now you're feeling like you not only should help, but have to.

But here's the thing—*just because you have the capacity doesn't mean it's your responsibility.*

Yes, you *can* still live up to your highest ideals, even while saying no to others in need.

Because if you fill all your downtime with others' needs, you won't give yourself the opportunity to recharge, process, and dream—all things needed for you to live a fulfilling life.

So next time you feel this way, take a step back and ask yourself if it truly makes sense for you right now.

I'm guessing most of the time, the answer will be no.

Ask Yourself This…
Am I regularly overextending myself for others at the expense of my own well-being, and if so, what boundaries can I set to ensure I take care of myself?

⸸ November 20

There's no lesson here.

Unsettled
I have that feeling.
You know, the one that keeps you up at night,
nervous, on-edge, and waiting for the morning
That low-level worry about *everything*.

Yes, there's impending change,
and maybe a few of those "top life stressors"
looming on the horizon.

So I'm writing this to keep my fingers moving,
my mind occupied, and my thoughts in check.
Maybe I'll get up and move too—
because both are a great way to move past this nervousness
and back into sleep.

I didn't think there would be a lesson here.
But if you can use movement and distraction the next time you're up in the middle of the night, then sharing this restless moment was definitely worth it.
This started off as just me, sharing this moment,
knowing that *you* would definitely understand.
And I truly hope you do

Ask Yourself This…
How can I find ways to soothe my unsettled thoughts when there's no clear answer or resolution in sight?

⸸ November 21

...there's too much to do that needs to be done.

No Time for Tears
I know, there's a lot to cry about. Really, I do.
There's serious stuff to deal with, and seemingly no way out.
And when you try to take that deep breath?
It feels like there's absolutely nowhere for it to go.
This is when, under "normal" circumstances,
you would break down, and the tears would start to flow.
But not now.

No, right now your body knows there's no time for tears,
and even less for the aftermath.

So while you secretly want the kind of deep release only tears can bring,
you know it's just not going to happen—
because there's too much that needs to be done,
and you know it's all up to you to do it.

If you're in this place right now, where the tears are
holding themselves back, and the weight of everything
you're dealing with isn't just on your shoulders,
but crushing you in ways you never thought possible—
just know that carrying this weight and bearing this burden in such a seemingly unsustainable way *just might be the most direct route out.*

So keep your head up, your shoulders square, and know that you were born with the strength to get through this.
Otherwise, all you'd be doing right now,
is crying.

Ask Yourself This...
When faced with tough situations, how do I find the strength to keep going?

⸸ November 22

...let life in.

Be Open
Be open to new people, places, things, thoughts, and experiences—
to unbridled joy, rising without fear of falling,
and trusting so deeply, it borders on faith.
Just be open. Because openness is the only way that the life
you were meant to live can ever unfold.

So please, just open the door a little bit
and *let life in.*

Ask Yourself This...
What is preventing me from being open to new things, and what can I do today to change that?

⸸ November 23

Let your worries out before bed.

Weight on Your Heart
Some days you wake up to a weight on your heart.
It's as if your troubles were crouched on your bedside,
just waiting to pounce before peace could place you gently in the day.

So you lie there, feeling like you never had a chance at a good day,
and it frustrates you all the more.
But what to do?

You process worry before you go to bed—
Just like I'm doing now.
It's not only cathartic but also preventative,
and will give you a much better shot at a
good night's sleep and a peaceful morning.

So let your worries out before bed.
Leave them on God's doorstep,
write them down, or share them with a friend.

Give them somewhere else to go.
And maybe in the morning,
they won't be crouched on your bedside table
Just waiting to pounce.

Ask Yourself This…
In what ways can I release worries before bed, and will I make this practice a regular part of my daily life?

November 24

Something bigger is happening.

You're Closer Than You Think
It might feel like you're a long way from your goals.
And maybe you are.
But trust me, you're closer than you think.

Why?
Because you're living every step in real time.
Every decision, success, setback, and pivot
stretches your sense of time, especially when it's new,
hard, or emotional.
That's why a day can feel like three, and a month forever.

But while you're down in the weeds figuring things out,
Something bigger is happening—
All the energy, passion, grit, and effort
you're pouring into your dream
is quietly moving you forward.
Not just on the timeline you see,
but in ways you'll never fully understand.

So keep going, especially when you feel like giving up.
Because it would be a shame to stop now,
when you're actually much closer than you think.

Ask Yourself This…
Isn't it time I took a step back and acknowledged how far I've come instead of focusing on how much I have left to do?

November 25

Give them Grace.

Grace
When someone is acting in ways you can't understand,
Give them Grace.

When someone is angry or sad,
Give them Grace.

When someone pushes in or through,
Give them Grace.

When someone doesn't move fast enough or goes too fast,
Give them Grace.

And when you see no reason at all why you should give someone grace, *definitely* give them Grace. Because they're probably the ones who need it most.

And please, never forget:
When you get angry…
When you're sad…
When you make mistakes…
When you feel like giving up…
When you decide not to…
When you're trying so hard to rise…
When you falter in the trying…
Then finally make it, but feel exhausted from the journey…
Give yourself Grace.

Because you deserve all the self-love, acceptance, and understanding, that comes along with it.

Ask Yourself This…
How can I make giving grace freely to myself and others a central part of my life?

⸸ November 26

... approach each day with the wonder of a child.

Life's In Control
With age comes the realization that life unfolds as it wishes—
on its own timeline and in its own way.

And for all our planning, obsessing, and illusion of control, we will always end up where life wants us at the very time it wants us there.

So do yourself a favor and try to approach each day with the wonder of a child who's experiencing life for the first time.

Because when you take off the blinders of expectation and *really* see what's around you, you'll discover that you actually are.

Every moment, laugh, tear, smile, step, and breathe is the first and the last of its kind.

So maybe it's time to reawaken to the wonder and truly see
where life is taking you.

Ask Yourself This…
What would I notice about my life today if I approached it not with control but complete curiosity?

⸸ November 27

...take the time for you, and nobody else.

Be Still Today
You have been stretched thin for far too long,
and are pulled constantly in every direction but inward.
So I think it's important for you to be still today.

To pause and reconnect with yourself on a deeper level.
To take the time *just for you*, and nobody else.

So today, find your center,
release as much as you can,
and go to that vulnerable place where your truth lives.
Not to blame, rehash, or judge,
but to heal.

You were born perfect—and you still are.
You were born enough—and you still are.
You were created to love.
And today, it begins again,
with you.

Ask Yourself This...
If not today, when will I make the time to center myself, release the weight of the world, and start to heal?

⚳ November 28

...please listen carefully to what your heart is saying.

Quote Your Own Heart
You can use the words of others to impress.
But the wisest words, the truest words,
the ones people really need to hear,
can only be said by you.

So today, please listen carefully to what your heart is saying,
then share it without hesitation.
Because when something so pure is said out loud,
the world instantly becomes,
a better place.

Ask Yourself This…
When will I finally trust in the fact that people truly do want to know my authentic self and that the words that come from my heart are the only ones I should be speaking?

⸸ November 29

It's time to be you.

The Things That Surface
That honesty.
That tear.
That "I love you."
That laughter.
That pain.
All that stuff that keeps trying to surface
but you keep pushing down.

It's time to let it break through,
see the light of day and be known.

It's time to breathe honest breaths,
speak words that are true,
and let the tears of joy and pain do what they do best:
Heal, release, and express what you're really feeling deep inside.

It's time to be you.
All you are and all you're meant to be.
So laugh, love, and live without apology.
The world has always needed the real you.
What a gift it would be,
to finally see it.

Ask Yourself This…
What things about myself am I keeping hidden from the world, and more importantly, why?

November 30

You are wise enough to truly live now.

Just right…
You're too old for this:
All the here and there,
the nonstop movement,
and the stress that comes with it all.

You're too young for this:
A life closing in,
walls going up,
and expectations coming down.

But you're just right for this:
Being centered and true.
Releasing the past,
and living in the now.

Because the now of you is perfect.
The now of you is whole.
And the now of you has seen enough to tell
the difference between a life worth living,
and a life less lived.

So yes, you are *finally*
whole enough,
wise enough,
and even old enough,
to truly live now.

So please take now,
and live.

Ask Yourself This…
What if my age isn't a barrier but a sweet spot, and how does that change things?

⚳ December 1

...life is a beautiful, messy mix, and so are you.

Some Days
Some days you will laugh,
others you will cry.

Some days you will love,
others you will not.

Some days you will eat healthy,
others you will eat junk.

Some days you will exercise,
others you will lay on the couch.

Some days you will live in the moment,
others you will worry about the future.

Some days you will find peace,
others you will be angry.

Some days you will live your purpose,
others, you will stray from it.

And that's all ok.
Because life is a beautiful, messy mix and so are you.
So keep trying, and keep growing.
Love your imperfections and never stop being
the beautiful, messy, imperfect human you are.

Ask Yourself This...
When will I finally accept my beautiful, messy self in all its imperfection, and live unapologetically as my true self?

December 2

So how many stones are at the bottom of your pool?

Stones in Pools
The stones of life enter with a splash,
making waves that bounce off the sides.
With time the waters calm.
and once again the surface looks like glass.

But the stones remain at the bottom.
Taking up space, scraping the skin off the feet
of anyone who comes near.
And are a worry that the owner knows
must be dealt with someday.

So my question for you is how many stones
are at the bottom of your pool?
And more importantly, when will you get them out?

Ask Yourself This…
How do my past experiences continue to impact my life, and when will I finally start to "remove the stones"?

⸸ December 3

...if you just slowed down.

Moments
Imagine how many more moments in your life you'd remember
if you
just.
slowed.
down.
enough.
to.
make.
them.
memorable.

Ask Yourself This...
How can I create space in my life to slow down and truly appreciate the everyday moments, and what can I do to make the simple things memorable?

⸸ December 4

We're all just figuring it out

Just So You Know…
You'll never have it *all* figured out.
Parts of it, of course,
but the whole thing?
Never.
So *please* stop beating yourself up for not having your life all figured out by now.
Because none of us do—
Not your doctor.
Not your successful friend.
And especially not "the experts".
We're all just figuring it out day by day.
And that's exactly how it's supposed to be.

Ask Yourself This…
Can I finally accept that everyone's winging it and start being honest that I am too?

⸸ December 5

...I'm right there with you.

We've Got This
You need to know that there's always someone else out there doing the same work, moving at a similar pace, and striving to make it happen just as much as you are.

So if you're feeling alone,
please know that I'm right here with you—
trying, succeeding, failing, and trying again.
Just like I'm supposed to.

So you and me?
We've got this.
Whatever "this" may be.

Let's go.

Ask Yourself This...
How can I remind myself on a daily basis that I'm not alone, even when things feel lonely?

⸸ December 6

This is what being in flow feels like.

Your Calling
When you feel called to do something, it feels much bigger than passion.
It's the feeling you get when things just "are."
Like a natural extension of yourself.

You live every waking moment in service of your dream.
You wake in the middle of the night with your mind in full gear,
and you feel unstoppable.

But feeling called to do something doesn't mean it will be easy—
expect a level of resistance that matches your enthusiasm,
to face seemingly impossible odds, and have people
you thought would support you doing the opposite.

But also expect a level of faith so unreasonable
you'll take all of that in stride.

This is what being in flow feels like—where ease and challenge blend together, elevating you toward something bigger than you ever imagined for yourself.

If any of this sounds familiar, then you *must* start now.
Write that page, make that call, and make it happen now.
Because the only way to derail yourself when you feel called,
is by hesitating.

Let's go.

Ask Yourself This...
Is there something I feel called to do? And if so, isn't it about time I answered?

⸸ December 7

So I closed my laptop.

The Light That Matters
The sun was rising as I was writing.
Deep in thought, playing with emotion,
trying to make things just right.

When out my window, I noticed the faint light.
too faint to compete with my screen,
And almost too subtle to be noticed.

So I closed my laptop.
And the sky exploded in light.
Shades of red, orange, silver, and gray,
layered brilliantly across the horizon.

And then it hit me.
We keep staring into the lights so bright that
the subtlety and softness of the world around us is lost.
We're focusing so much on what we've created for ourselves,
that we've shut out the true masterpiece that surrounds us every day.

So isn't it about time we looked up from our screens,
and started paying attention to the light that matters most?

Ask yourself this…
When was the last time I closed my laptop or put down my phone to simply experience what was around me, and shouldn't I do it more?

⸸ December 8

Joy will surely follow.

Becoming Joyful
It starts with the awareness of the blessings in your life,
whether they be large, small, or even microscopic.
Gratitude for them comes next—
and when repeated daily, turns to joy.

But becoming a "joyful person" takes more
than just a "gratitude practice."

You have to believe it, go all in, and allow yourself to be so *amazed* at the abundance in your life (and there is abundance no matter who you are), that you couldn't stop the joy from pouring out of you if you tried.

I know, it sounds like a lot of work,
but wouldn't it be worth your while to at least give it a try?
And really, what do you have to lose—
Sadness?

Ask Yourself This…
What are three things I am genuinely grateful for in my life right now, no matter how big, small, or even microscopic?

♇ December 9

You'll feel more alive, supported, and connected.

Inside Out

Sometimes, you get the rare opportunity to meet someone from the inside out. To be in a space—or a moment—where it feels safe, or necessary, to drop your defenses, and speak honestly about your life with a stranger in a way you never thought possible.

That's where the magic lives.
Because when you first meet the *person*, not the *persona,*
you immediately realize just how alike we all are at the deepest levels.

I've had that opportunity, and the result is much of what you're now holding in your hands.

So if you ever get the chance to show up fully, get vulnerable,
and meet someone from the inside out—take it.

You'll feel more supported and connected than you ever thought possible. And who knows, maybe something great will come from it. Maybe even a book of your own.

Ask Yourself This…

Where can I find courses, groups, or events that will give me the opportunity to meet people from the inside out?

⸸ December 10

Perhaps loneliness isn't a path but a space.

Loneliness

Loneliness is a difficult path to walk,
and it often leads to places you don't want to go.

But I wonder—
If you focused on finding purpose instead on companionship,
would the like-minded people you've been looking for
naturally start to appear?

So maybe, what you see as a void is actually just a *space*—
one for other purpose-driven people to fill
once you start moving in the direction of yours.

So if you're feeling alone,
the question isn't, "Who will walk with me?"
but, "Where am I meant to go?"
Your answers—and the people you've been looking for—
just might meet you there.

Ask Yourself This…

What can I do today to shift my focus from being lonely to following my interests and passions that lead me towards my purpose?

⸸ December 11

**I hope today is sweet, kind,
and gentle with you.**

**And when it's done,
That you have something you can
look back on, and smile.**

⸸ December 12

I knew I had what it took to get through.

Brutally Honest

Before you begin the journey toward the life you want,
you need to stop and be brutally honest with yourself.
Now, when I said that, did you think I meant making a list of all the things you need to fix or overcome before anything good could happen in your life? Because I actually meant the opposite.

When things were falling apart for me in 2016/17,
I spent a lot of time beating myself up over the decisions I'd made.
I was stuck, paralyzed by fear, terrified to take the next step because I'd lost trust in myself.

Then one night, while drowning in self-pity over the woes that had befallen me (yes, it felt that dramatic), I started listing everything that had gone wrong over the years.

When out of nowhere, an image of a mountain popped into my mind—one made of all the trials, failures, missteps, and challenges I'd been replaying in my head.

Then it hit me:
Not only had I climbed that mountain, but had conquered it, and with far less experience than I have now.

That changed everything.
When I compared that mountain to what I was facing at the time,
my current challenges suddenly seemed small.
I knew I had what it took to get through—because I had proof.

So before you take your next step, think about all the times you've been tested, all the things you've overcome, and all the times you felt you didn't have anything left to take the next step

But you did anyway.
Dig deep and make the list as long—and honest—as you can.
That's your mountain.

Now step back and celebrate that you made it to the top.
Sure, you've got some scars and bruises showing,
and maybe there's still more to work through.

But more importantly, you also have the lessons they left behind—
the ones that will pave your way forward.

Let's be real—
You and I both know you have what it takes to overcome what you're going through, because if you didn't, you wouldn't even be thinking about taking the first step on the path forward..

So, be brutally honest with yourself and get going up the trail,
because all the proof you need is already waiting for you—
right there at the top of your mountain.

Ask Yourself This...
What have I already conquered that proves I have the strength to face what lies ahead?

⸸ December 13

You have a soundtrack of your own...

Background Music
Have you ever noticed how profoundly the background music impacts the meaning of a film? Those subtle, almost imperceptible sounds that exist just below the surface—the ones you can't quite describe but *feel*?

And did you ever consider that you have a soundtrack of your own?
It's that voice inside your head. The one continuously streaming negative self-talk, and framing your perspective on every word, action, and move you make.

So what kind of movie are you currently watching?
And more importantly—
Isn't it time to change the soundtrack?

Ask Yourself This...
How can I use the movie soundtrack analogy to notice when my inner narrative doesn't align with the life I'm trying to create?

⳩ December 14

...take a breath and see life for what it truly is.

What Life Wants
Life wants to wrap you in its arms.
Show you why you're here and what it came to teach you.

Life is kind.
And if you let it,
it will guide you along your path in the only way it knows how—
always with your best interest in mind.

But somewhere along the line,
you were taught that life is hard, cruel, and relentless.
That it doesn't want to teach, but to break you.
And you started looking for proof of that,
turning life's lessons into evidence of cruelty.
And that's a tragedy.
Because it's made you look at life with a wary eye
instead of an open heart.
And that, more than anything,
may be what's keeping you from the simple, joyful life you long for.

So today, take a breath.
See life for what it truly is—
an invitation for your heart to play, dance, and sing.
For your mind to learn and grow.
And for your soul to take it all in,
turning every moment into the wisdom
that will guide you toward the happiness
you were born to experience.

Ask Yourself This...
What if life is here to love you, guide you, and teach you—and always has been?

⸸ December 15

Life is meant to be enjoyed, one moment at a time.

The Gift
There is joy, wonder, and inspiration
packed into every second of life.
But you can access only by living
one. moment. at. a. time.

It's comes from actively looking for blessings
in the ordinary acts of living,
and keeping your heart and mind open to what could be.

So stop and look around *right now*—
is there something or someone near you
that proves what I'm saying?
Maybe a gift you've been overlooking,
or a simple moment waiting to be enjoyed?

I think it's a good idea for you to slow down.
open your heart, and finally accept this shift toward happiness.
Because once you do,
it will be impossible to go back.

Ask Yourself This…
Who or what around me might be a gift I've overlooked? How can I finally accept what they have to give?

⸸ December 16

...the weight that there's no scale for.

Invisible Weight

There's an invisible weight we all carry.
A weight for which there's no scale,
that can't be measured,
and it is harder to lose than those last 5 pounds.
And you could say it's the weight that matters most.

I'm talking about the weight on your heart.
The weight of worry, stress, pain, fear, burden, regret, and judgment.
The weight you truly need to lose to look, feel, and be your best.

Just like those last 5 pounds,
It takes time, consistency, effort, and self-awareness.
But most of all, it takes desire.
So the question is, are you ready to do what it takes?
To start the breathing, healing, moving, and actions it will take
to finally shed the weight that's been holding you down?
And if not, why?

Ask Yourself This…

How has carrying this invisible weight affected my relationships, personal growth, and overall sense of fulfillment?

⸸ December 17

Can you tell me where you're going?

Racing to Nowhere

Where are you racing to—
with your blood pressure raised,
shoulders tight, and breath short?
Can you tell me where you're going, and why it's worth it?

Maybe you have an answer.
Maybe there's some near or distant future
that you believe is worth the sacrifice.

But what if you never stop, only to realize someday
that the destination you thought would finally make you happy, *never truly existed*?
Think about that.

Ask Yourself This…

Do you ever stop to question what the goal is of your constant hustle and if it's all truly worth it?

⸸ December 18

kinda like you…

Beautiful Things
I love things of quality.
Beautiful, one-of-a-kind things—
ones that took patience, effort, and time to create.
Special, amazing, and breathtaking things.
Things, well, kinda like you…

Ask Yourself This…
In what ways am I beautiful and unique, and how can I develop a deeper sense of self-appreciation?

December 19

...please know that you're not alone.

The Other Side of Merry
If you're going through a rough time—
if the lights aren't so bright this year,
and you find yourself on the other side of merry—
Please know that you're not alone.

While many may smile simply for the sake of the season,
please remember you are under no obligation to do the same.

Life can be hard.
And can be even harder when you're expected
to carry nothing but joy in your heart every day.

So if you're hurting and this time of year brings you down,
give yourself permission to do whatever you need to get through—
including saying no to the activities, parties, and gatherings
you feel obligated to attend.

Because at the end of the day,
doing something that drains you in the name of celebration
is the last thing you need.

So be strong,
take care of yourself,
and know that brighter, lighter days
are coming your way.

Ask Yourself This...
Can I have the courage to protect my mental and emotional well-being by saying no to the things I've always felt obligated to do, and if not, why?

⸸ December 20

Expect to have fun.

How to have a great time at a party (and succeed at life)

1. Drink plenty of water before you leave the house.
2. Take the time to look your best.
3. Expect to have fun.
4. Smile a lot.
5. Drop your judgment and go with the flow.
6. Relax and be loose (but don't be a fool).
7. Seek out interesting conversations.
8. Avoid the things you'll regret tomorrow.
9. Be grateful you're there.
10. Step back for a minute just to take it all in.

... And if that song's not your jam, don't fake it—just get off the dance floor!

Ask Yourself This…

How would my life change if I just did everything on this list for a month?

⸸ December 21

...But what once was, is no more.

The Rhythm of Life
There once was a rhythm, a flow, a predictability to life—
After-school play.
Dinner at 5.
Homework.
Tuesday night TV.
Bedtime.

It was safe, comfortable, and simple.
In the mundane came slow growth and connection.
In boredom, imaginative thought.
And in the space to simply breathe, self-awareness.

But what once was is no more.
Now it feels like we're binge-watching life,
instead of experiencing it bit by bit and day by day.

The question I have today isn't how we got here
or even return, but create a new version of what life should be.
One where true connection with the ones we love is valued above everything, and spent in pursuit of that cadence, balance, and harmony we so deeply miss.

So here's the real question:
How can we take what we've learned
and create that new version of life—
one that our kids will one day look back upon
And smile?

Ask Yourself This…

How do I do my part to create that cadence and connection I so desperately need right now?

⸸ December 22

It's in those moments when we've been harmed that we can only pray grace takes the place of anger and forgiveness that of blame.

I Was Rear-Ended… This Is What I Learned

We were stopped at a red light. A woman, with a 3-year-old in her car, was distracted and never hit the brake.
Our lives suddenly collided at 40 mph.

My mind went from autopilot—
foot on the brake, waiting for the light to change, sorting through unconscious thoughts—to the lightning-fast progression of shock:
Fear that my son was hurt.
Fear that I was hurt.
Relief that we were both breathing.
Shock that this had happened.
Worry we'd be hit again.
Relief to see everything had stopped behind us.
I worried when I saw the other car completely demolished.
A decision to check on the other driver.
Concern for my son.
Empathy for how he was feeling.
Responsibility to give him instruction.
And then, the action of leaving the car.

My worry and concern quickly turned to relief when I saw that she was okay—
but then to anger when I noticed her phone (which she denied using).

As soon as anger surfaced, I instinctively went back to my car.
Anger is a useless emotion in a crisis—it only makes things worse.
And I'm grateful I had the presence of mind to act on that instinct.

Once grace replaced the anger, I returned to check on her again.
That's when I saw the child in the car seat.

This mom had made not only a mistake, but also one with her child in the car.
I realized there was no anger or blame I could give her that could match what she was already giving herself—and forgiveness appeared.

I know if things had been worse, forgiveness may not have come so quickly—or even at all—but I'm glad it did.

The whole ordeal took four hours, from the moment we were hit to leaving the emergency room.
We're both really uncomfortable (and I think we'll need a new car based on the damage), but I'm thankful the vehicles absorbed most of the impact, and it seems like everyone involved will be okay.

I don't know why our lives collided last night.
I don't know why her distraction became my physical pain,
or her hurriedness my new financial burden.

Maybe she needed that moment of primal fear to change her perspective on life.
Maybe I needed it to gain some perspective on the pain in mine.
Regardless of the reason, all we can do is learn what we can from this and move on.

Stay safe out there.

Ask Yourself This…
How do I react in moments of upheaval, and is there anything in this experience that calls me to handle situations like this differently?

⸸ December 23

Are you ready?

Are You Really Ready?
If you're waiting for January 1st to change your life,
odds are you're simply not ready.
Real change happens when the status quo is truly *no longer an option.*

So, don't just ask yourself if you *want* to change,
ask if you're *ready* to—
because if you're not truly ready,
it will all just be a massive waste of time.
So be honest—
Are you ready?

Ask Yourself This…
Have I reached the point where the status quo is TRULY no longer an option?

⸸ December 24

Without a doubt, you should be.

I Hope You're Proud of Yourself
I hope you're proud of yourself for the amazing person you are,
And for making the world a better place.

I hope you're proud of yourself for facing life's challenges,
and being there every day for the people who rely on you.

I hope you're proud of yourself for learning and growing,
and becoming a better version of yourself with each new day.

I hope you're proud of yourself for the laughter you've shared,
and the joy you've spread and the happiness you've sparked in others.

I hope you're proud of yourself for the love you've given,
and the friendships you've built along the way.

I hope you're proud of yourself for staying true to your values,
and standing up for what you believe in.

I hope you're proud of yourself for dreaming big,
and taking those steps to bring them to life.

I hope you're proud of yourself for facing the unknown with courage,
and continuing to write your own story.

But above all, I hope you're proud of yourself simply for the person you are, what you bring to the world, and the incredible difference you make, just by being you. Because without a doubt,
you should be.

Ask Yourself This…
What's your list of the things you're proud of yourself for?

⸸ December 25

…just keep trying.

Imperfect

You may be trying to live a perfect life.
With your perfect house
manicured lawn
and picture-perfect family.

And you may be proud of how it all looks,
what it says about you
and the life you've built.

But here's the thing—
You weren't born to live a perfect life.
You were born to try, to fail, to learn, and to try again.

And I know you're doing that.
But in your case, maybe the weight of "Perfect"
Is holding you down more than you realize.

So please
Put down the perfect, and pick up the beautifully flawed.
Because authenticity looks better on everyone.
And I think it would look especially good on you.

Ask Yourself This…

Will putting down the perfect be possible for me, and if not, how can I get there?

⸸ December 26

What am I willing to change to make this happen?

Make New Year's Priorities, Not Resolutions
You can't have your existing life *and* the life you want.
For everything you add, something must go.
So if you've made that list of resolutions and goals,
take a moment to look at it again and ask yourself,
"What am I willing to change to make this happen?"

In that honesty, you'll discover whether your resolution is truly the gateway to a better life, or merely a fleeting desire you're not yet ready to fully embrace.

Ask Yourself This…
What am I willing to change to ensure that I prioritize what's truly important in my life?

⸸ December 27

Are you with me?

Next Year
I'm not planning on "crushing" next year.
I'm simply going to take it one day at a time,
do my best, and accept whatever comes my way
with as much grace as I can.
Are you with me?

Ask Yourself This…
Can I finally accept that doing my best is good enough, regardless of how things turn out?

⸸ December 28

It will take everything you have.

Smolder

When it comes to transformation,
it's about the smolder, not the burn.
It's about showing up for yourself first,
accepting who you are at your core, and celebrating it
without exception, and unbounded by rules.
There will be no comparisons to "normal" and no holds barred.
This is serious and must not be taken lightly.

This will also be a practice—
One that will take you deep into your past and even your soul.
Not searching for what needs to be fixed,
but for what needs to be nurtured, cared for, and grown.

It's about a commitment to physical, mental, and emotional health,
to friendships based on mutual interests and passions,
and honoring those relationships the best you can.

It will take deconstruction and a commitment to slow down,
be present, and step into the person you've been constructing your entire life.

But above all, it will be worth it.
because deep down, you know—
It's time.

Ask Yourself This...

Am I ready to do the work required to look critically at, deconstruct, and rebuild myself in a way that is truest to who I am at my very core? If not, why?

December 29

Treat others as if they're going through the worst thing you've ever experienced.

Ask Yourself This…
How can I change my thinking so that I am more understanding and empathetic towards others in the moment, no matter what?

♆ December 30

Do this, and your road to recovery will be short.

The Advice You Give
Sometimes you're asked to be there for others,
so you listen intently, and bring as much love as you can.
You offer advice that comes purely from a place of wanting to help—
advice that pulls on every last bit of your experience and flows straight from your heart.

Then one day, you'll find yourself needing someone to show up for you with advice of their own.
It is at these moments that it's wise to look not to others first,
But go back to the advice you've given in the past, tapping into that inner wisdom you shared when it was coming from a place of service, not desperation.

There you'll find the most brilliant advice you could ever hope for, because it came directly from your soul while operating in a place of pure love for another.

Once you've done this, don't hesitate to ask for help—
Ask friends, family, and even strangers. Share the opportunity to serve, solve, and help with as many as you need. By doing this, your road out of where you are will be much shorter than if you simply tried,
to go it alone.

Ask Yourself This…
How does the thought of applying the wisdom I've shared with others to navigate my own challenges make me feel? Does it make sense, and if not, why?

⸸ December 31

I'm guessing it doesn't feel quite right.

Never Regret Kindness

Have you ever done something kind, only to regret it moments later? Maybe you went out of your way to say something nice that didn't land as intended, or gave your money or time to someone you quickly realized was manipulating you.

You probably felt foolish,
and vowed never to let that happen again.
Then maybe you put your guard up, complimented less,
and said "no" more often, which sadly that became a habit that still exists today.

And somehow, you've become fine with it.

But here's the thing, by retreating you let just one or two bad experiences close off the most beautiful part of you—
your ability to recognize opportunities for kindness
and offer it in an increasingly unkind world.

So here you are with your open heart closed,
your desire to spread kindness stifled,
and a part of your soul unfulfilled—
And I'm guessing it doesn't feel quite right.

So I ask you to never regret showing kindness again,
because it will hurt not only you, but all the people who will feel seen and cared for, by the ripple effect of your love.

Ask Yourself This…

Does this ring true for you in terms of being less open, kind, and giving? And if so, can you please start again?

About the Author

Ed Goyette is a lifelong social entrepreneur driven by a passion for enriching the lives of others. With *Thoughtuary*, he brings his signature blend of personal reflection and practical wisdom to life. Inspired by his deep love for kayaking and the clarity found on the water, *Thoughtuary* offers a daily sanctuary for the mind—guiding readers to navigate their thoughts and build a more intentional life.

Ed is the Co-founder of *Major Choice*, a mentorship-based career exploration program that empowers students with disabilities to uncover their strengths and confidently plan for the future. His entrepreneurial spirit also shines through *BeanTowne Coffee House*, a nationally award-winning café established in 1993 that continues today in New Hampshire. Previously, he launched *Yours for the Asking*, a program that helps parents strengthen relationships with their children by nurturing curiosity through the art of asking.

A recognized thought leader, Ed is a TEDx speaker and Global Presence Ambassador for one of the world's largest parenting organizations. He is a proud husband and father of three, who remain a constant source of inspiration in both his work and life.

⸸ INDEX

www.ingramcontent.com/pod-product-compliance
Lightning Source LLC
Chambersburg PA
CBHW072107270326
41931CB00010B/1477